Routledge Library Editions

ECONOMICS AND SOCIOLOGY

ECONOMICS

Routledge Library Editions – Economics

METHODOLOGY & PHILOSOPHY OF ECONOMICS
In 5 Volumes

I	Economics and Economic Policy in Britain, 1946-1966	*Hutchison*
II	'Positive' Economics and Policy Objectives	*Hutchison*
III	Economics and Sociology	*Löwe*
IV	Economic Doctrine and Method	*Schumpeter*
V	Lament for Economics	*Wootton*

ECONOMICS AND SOCIOLOGY

A Plea for Co-Operation in the Social Sciences

ADOLF LÖWE

Routledge
Taylor & Francis Group
LONDON AND NEW YORK

First published in 1935

Reprinted in 2003 by
Routledge
2 Park Square, Milton Park, Abingdon, Oxon, OX14 4RN
or
270 Madison Avenue, New York, NY 10016

First issued in paperback 2010

Routledge is an imprint of the Taylor & Francis Group

British Library Cataloguing in Publication Data
A CIP catalogue record for this book
is available from the British Library

Economics and Sociology
ISBN 978-0-415-31388-9 (hbk)
ISBN 978-0-415-60798-8 (pbk)
ISBN 978-0-415-31385-8 (set)

Miniset: Methodology & Philosophy of Economics

Series: Routledge Library Editions – Economics

Economics and Sociology

A PLEA FOR CO-OPERATION
IN THE SOCIAL SCIENCES

by

Dr. Adolf Löwe

Hon. Research Fellow in the University of Manchester; formerly Professor of Economics in the Universities of Kiel and Frankfurt am Main

WITH A FOREWORD BY

Morris Ginsberg

Martin White Professor of Sociology in the University of London

Routledge
Taylor & Francis Group
LONDON AND NEW YORK

Published 1935

TO

FRANZ OPPENHEIMER

AND

KARL MANNHEIM

SUCCESSIVE HOLDERS OF THE CHAIR OF SOCIOLOGY IN THE GOETHE-UNIVERSITÄT OF FRANKFURT AM MAIN

1919-1933

A PERIOD OF CONSTRUCTIVE SYNTHESIS IN THE SOCIAL SCIENCES

CONTENTS

PREFACE

This study originated in three Public Lectures delivered at the University of London, London School of Economics and Political Science, in February 1935. Though the text has been revised and considerably extended in some parts the character of the lecture-form has been retained. Only within the loose and unpretentious frame of the original do I venture to approach a wider public with a very short and sometimes rather aphoristic treatment of problems which might well fill several big books. I hope in the near future to present a more detailed exposition of some problems of dynamic economics which have been touched upon in this essay.

For valuable suggestions as to form and content I am much indebted to Professor Karl Mannheim, now at the London School of Economics and Political Science, Professor J. L. Stocks, of the University of Manchester, Mr. A. P. Lerner of the London School of Economics and Political Science, and Dr. Gerhard Meyer, of the International Institute of Social Research, Paris. Mrs. Elsa Sinclair, M.A., Ph.D., took upon herself the task of combating my Teutonisms and even worse mistakes. I also have to thank the University of London for its grant towards the expenses of publication.

It is impossible for me to mention by name all those persons and institutions whose generosity has made it possible for me to submit any publication at all. But my thanks go out to them, among them especially the Faculty of Commerce and Administration in the Victoria University of Manchester and the Rockefeller Foundation.

ADOLF LÖWE.

Manchester,

June 1935.

FOREWORD

The substance of this book was contained in a series of three lectures delivered by Dr. Löwe at the London School of Economics under the University scheme of advanced lectures in sociology. They were deeply appreciated by the students of economics and sociology to whom they were primarily addressed. In re-writing them for a wider public Dr. Löwe has kindly invited me to provide a short introduction, and I welcome the opportunity thus afforded me of expressing my gratitude to him, and the hope which, I am sure, will be shared by all students of sociology, that his work will help in bringing about that closer co-operation between the social sciences for which he here makes so powerful an appeal.

The issues raised by Dr. Löwe are of old standing, and it may be of interest to inquire how far the attitude taken by economists to sociology at the time of its infancy is justified in the light of later developments. We may consider first of all the position of J. S. Mill, who though extremely sympathetic to sociology as a synthetic science of society and though as deeply imbued as Comte with what he described as the consensus of social phenomena, that is the close interrelation of all parts of social life, nevertheless regarded political economy as a distinct and separate branch of sociological speculation. As the points made by him, especially in the sixth book of the *Logic*, are still, in essentials, in the centre of discussion, it may be useful to define his attitude more clearly. The relative independence of political economy was due, in his opinion, to the fact that the phenomena with which it is concerned depended *mainly* upon one class of causes, namely those that act through the psychological law that a greater gain is preferred to a smaller, counteracted only by the " aversion to labour and the desire of the present enjoyment of costly indulgences ". He thought that, arguing deductively from these assumptions, results could be arrived at which would retain their importance even though they might turn out to require qualification when they were used in the interpretation of concrete phenomena. It is, however, to be remembered that though he thus defended the value of economics as a self-contained discipline, he also laid great stress on the need of studying these possible modifying influences, especially those arising out of differences in class structure and out of differences in national characteristics. He advocated the establishment of a science of ethology, that is to say, of group psychology, and he pointed out that in the absence of such a science economists were apt to assume as universal laws of human nature regularities of behaviour, such as a certain form of competitiveness, which were in fact only verified, if at all, for countries like Great Britain and the United States. Indeed he goes so far as to say that the more highly the science of national character is cultivated, the smaller will the number of propositions become which could be safely regarded as universal principles of human nature. Nevertheless he was of the opinion that these diversities of national character only affected economic behaviour in a secondary degree. Consequently, while he would not allow independent status to the science of politics, on the ground that the latter was concerned with problems in which national characteristics were involved at every step, he maintained that economics was sufficiently self-contained to justify its claims to constitute a separate, though not independent, branch of social inquiry. Since Mill's time the study of social psychology has made some progress, but it must be admitted that the branches of psychology concerned with national groups have hardly attained sufficient maturity for their conclusions to be of immediate service to economics. To what extent, for example, do the mental habits of Frenchmen, Englishmen and Germans affect the economic structure of their countries? How far was the history of colonization shaped on its economic side by differences in the mentality of the Dutch, Spaniards, Frenchmen and Englishmen? In what ways are changes in the general standard of life brought about by non-economic factors and what influence is exerted by these upon the level of prices and wages? What role is played in international trade by national differences in inertia and the forces of tradition? These are all problems upon which existing social psychology throws but little light. Here it seems to me social psychologists are at least as much at fault as the economists. There is great need for co-operation between them if only for the purpose of enabling them to understand each other's problems.

Later discussions of the methodology of the social sciences seized on the points made by Mill and Comte, notably the complexity and interrelatedness of social phenomena and the dangers of the abstract or deductive methods. But English economists do not appear to have been greatly interested in or impressed by this struggle about methods. Marshall pointed out very early in his career that the complexity and intricacy of social phenomena afforded no reason for dispensing with the economic organon, and that, on the contrary, they increased the necessity for it. Without in any way minimizing the importance of realistic studies, he urged that "facts by themselves are silent" and that in order to yield results of value they must be subjected to the technique gradually perfected by economic theory. His attitude to sociology was more trenchant. "It is vain," he said in his Inaugural Lecture in 1885, "to speak of the higher authority of a unified social science. No doubt if that existed economics would gladly find shelter under its wings. But it does not exist; it shows no signs of coming into existence. There is no use in waiting idly for it; we must do what we can with our present resources." Somewhat similar is the view developed in the same year by Sidgwick in his Presidential address to the section on Economic Science and Statistics of the British Association. Without denying the possibility of a science of society, he felt that the results so far achieved by sociologists were not sufficiently definite or reliable to afford material help to political economy.

Sociology, Sidgwick argued, does not stand the tests of a real science, namely consensus or continuity and power of prevision. The leading sociological treatises available in his day, the works of Spencer, Comte and Schäffle, exhibited, he thought, the most conspicuous absence of agreement or continuity in their treatment of the fundamental questions of social evolution, and their predictions of the future of religion or of industrial development sharply contradicted each other. Sociology struck him as nothing better than a mixture of vague analogies, imperfectly verified historical generalizations and unwarranted political predictions. When it had passed out of this rudimentary condition it would be time for economists to come to terms with it. Meanwhile they had better carry on their confessedly limited but thereby more manageable inquiries in as scientific a manner as possible. The ultimate value of sociology or its possibility need not be disputed. What is called in question is its helpfulness in its then very imperfect stage of development. Has the position changed fundamentally after the lapse of half a century? Are Sidgwick's remarks applicable, say, to the sociology of Durkheim, Max Weber or Hobhouse? Such questions must be faced by anyone who, like Dr. Löwe, pleads for co-operation between sociology and economics; the need for such co-operation is clear, but can sociologists deliver the goods?

An examination of the work of the distinguished sociologists just referred to will show, I think, that all of them have contributed much of value towards the theory of the general development of society, and that all have developed methods for the study of the relations between the various factors of social life, which, though not identical, complement each other. It seems to me also that they do provide a useful starting point for a theory of social causation and for evaluating the role played by economic forces in the growth of society. Further, the growth of the sociology of knowledge and especially the considerable development of the comparative study of social institutions, of religious and moral beliefs and practices, which has taken place during the last half century, ought to be of service in supplementing and enriching the work of the economists. In particular, these studies ought to afford help in answering the question whether the economic laws which have been established are universal but work out differently under different conditions, or whether they are laws which merely state the consequences of conditions peculiar to particular societies or civilizations. The business of sociology in relation to economics is not to minimize, or to seek to displace, economic analysis, but rather to throw light on the conditions under which the laws propounded as a result of economic analysis work, and, in this respect, modern sociology surely deserves more consideration than was shown it by its early critics.

That economics can render valuable aid to sociology is equally clear. Dr. Löwe has shown this in his extremely illuminating discussion of the claims of historical materialism, but it is impressed on the sociologist in all his efforts to deal with the major problems of civilization. The study of the phenomena connected with urbanization, for example, cannot proceed very far without paying attention to the effects of changes in the technique of industry and agriculture and their influence upon mobility and the ratio of urban to rural inhabitants. The sociological aspects of the problems of population can hardly be dissevered from the economic. The investigation of the changes which are occurring in the family, in governmental organization, in the growth of the various forms of nationalism, raises questions which cannot be fruitfully explored without a full examination of the interplay between economic and socio-political forces. The modern sociologist has not only to be familiar with the principal results of economic theory, but he ought also to have sufficient command of the technique of economic analysis to enable him to bring these results into relation with the conclusions reached by him in his own investigations. Dr. Löwe's work affords an excellent example of what can be achieved by one who is equally equipped in both disciplines towards the constructive synthesis which he here advocates and of which he has so fully shown the need. With all modern sociologists he realizes clearly that a fruitful synthesis can only be achieved with the aid of the specialisms which the division of labour has necessarily brought into being. There are many indications in recent work that these specialisms are being increasingly influenced by the sociological point of view. Sociologists can encourage this tendency by freeing their discipline from the charge of vagueness and by proving their capacity to utilize the results of the specialists in a manner which they can respect, while at the same time contributing to the more inclusive interpretation of society which is the professed task of sociology.

MORRIS GINSBERG.

London School of Economics.

CHAPTER I

A PLAIN APPROACH TO THE PROBLEM

I

ACADEMIC research in the social sciences and the practical application of their results are suffering to-day from a general defect for which even the greatest achievements within the special branches cannot compensate. An excessive division of labour, a lack of synthetic co-operation between the various sections of social research more and more restrict the truth of any partial knowledge, the efficiency of any concrete action. Some practical examples will lead us into the centre of the problem better than lengthy methodological reflections.

In the autumn of 1923, the German inflation was stopped with the help of the so-called Rentenmark. Almost every monetary expert and financial authority had been strongly opposed to the introduction of that new type of currency. From the viewpoint of purely economic reasoning the additional emission of more than 2,000 millions Rentenmark, equivalent to more than 100 millions gold pounds, could hardly be supposed to restore stability of the monetary system but rather to expand inflation. Absurd ideas on the backing of the new currency by a general mortgage on the industrial and agricultural property of the country could not but destroy the last vestige of public confidence in monetary management. But as there was no other practicable plan, the project was rushed through by the bureaucracy of the treasury, and developed into one of the most sensational successes of economic policy in modern history.

What had happened? Was the education in economics and the experience of some politicians and government officials so much superior to the views of the vast majority of industrialists, bankers and professors? But if not, if the better argument was with the pessimists, what are we to think of a science the advice of which does not prove practical when most needed?

The economist will reply that the German policy of stabilization has certainly not succeeded because of the general ideas on currency and monetary management held by its promoters. The success is to be attributed to the co-operation of many non-monetary, even non-economic factors but psychological and political ones, the accidental rise of which made up for the bad effect of the monetary measures. A superstitious belief of the masses in the mystery of backing a currency by real values, the devaluation of the monetary unit down to the pre-war level—a loaf of bread suddenly again costing 50 Pfennige instead of 500 milliards Mark—the general demand for any means of circulation at all, these and other facts established new confidence among the public. In this way money's average velocity of circulation was reduced, foreign currency more and more driven out of the internal circuit, and a space was opened for the infiltration of new currency.

Certainly the collective action of all those factors could not be precalculated by mere economic reasoning, and the wrong monetary ideas of the bureaucracy do not become right all at once, after some accidental events have checked the bad results of a dubious policy. What, however, do we positively mean by calling those ultimately decisive factors "accidental"? Obviously we mean that from the economist's point of view there is no general rule in the rise and course of these meta-economic events. But is it not the essence of every monetary system that it cannot function except on the basis of definite ideologies or certain expectations as to the future policy of the authorities and as to the behaviour of the members of the community? It has been proved by history that the general public reacts in a typical manner to different monetary manipulations. We might easily collect these experiences and systematize them into a sociology and psychology of money, of credit, of inflation and deflation. As economists we may not feel competent to deal with such problems. But are there not other sciences explicitly dealing with mass-psychology, social prejudices, public opinion, etc., sciences which may long ago have discovered the corresponding rules of human behaviour? After we have once realized that rational monetary policy must be based on two pillars—on the economics as well as on the social psychology of money—why leave it to the amateurs in politics and administration to combine superficial economic ideas with everyday psychology, instead of rendering social science applicable by scientific co-operation?

Take another example. Right from the beginning when economics formed itself as an autonomous science, historians, lawyers, sociologists opposed the constitution of pure economics. They pointed out that every economic process, even the freest play of forces in the market, rests on some definite legal institutions, above all on property rights expressing the class structure and determining how the agents of production are to be disposed of.

That is certainly true. But is it the whole truth? Is the lawyer and the sociologist really the superior authority, when the creation of wealth and the changes in class-structure of our society are to be investigated? After all it was the economic process itself, its recurrent cycle of good and bad trade which during the nineteenth century has proved to be the mightiest force in creating wealth and in redistributing property, which has overthrown the traditional aristocracy of the past and enthroned a new leading class. In other words: the historian, the lawyer, the sociologist though indispensable collaborators in the field of realistic economics, cannot deal with their own special problems such as the dynamics of modern society, the substantial significance of the legal forms and the ultimate basis of the class-order, if they are not familiar with the economic theories of the trade cycle, of entrepreneur's profit, investment and decapitalization.

We are told there was once an age when only the state was administered by bureaucrats, while economic enterprise was in the hands of versatile independent-minded people trained in the struggle of competition, well conscious of their economic chances and at their best if left to their own devices. Frederick the Great 150 years ago was of another opinion. He thought, as he wrote on the margin of one of his edicts, that the plebs—so he called the Commons—will not keep from the humdrum tune, unless you drag them by their noses and ears to their profits. That may be somewhat out of date ; but has our modern large-scale organization not removed much of the former difference between public administration and private enterprise ? We cannot come to any practical conclusions on the problems of monopoly, tariffs or technical progress, without accommodating our argument to the changes in economic psychology, in the working incentive, even in the general conception of life. There is no realistic theory of costs without definite ideas as to the role, which security, progress, leisure play in the mind of the leading as well as of the dependent groups. But at the same time we shall never understand continental parliamentarianism and the breakdown of German and Italian democracy, unless we realize that political parties in these countries, lacking any democratic tradition, tried to handle government and parliament as they were accustomed to handle a meeting of shareholders or a business transaction. We have got to study modern business behaviour in order to understand modern politics, and we cannot understand economic dynamics, if we are not familiar with the patterns of life in other social spheres.

II

Emphasis on synthetic problems and on co-operation in solving them must not be interpreted as if we underestimated the familiar problems of economics or the important specialist work of anthropologists and sociologists, lawyers and historians. However, it is not theoretical caprice but the epoch-making transformation of our social reality which no longer allows us to restrict our investigations to the mere refinements of our textbook problems. The present-day complexes of our political and economic practice, imperialism, the crisis of democracy, education in citizenship, social and economic planning, do not fit into the watertight compartments of our traditional systems of specialisms. Even if some dislike the substance of these problems and the age that has brought them about, if they personally prefer the former order of well specialized human activities and scientific aspects, we cannot help dealing with social reality as it is, not only deeply entangled, but dependent on rational unfolding for its mere persistence.

Certainly there are many good reasons for academic reserve in these discussions. All problems arising from the intermingling of various social spheres are so very complicated that hardly any definite answer can be obtained to-day. And wherever science has any solution to offer, it will not and cannot be so plain, and in most cases not so pleasant to private interests and personal prejudices as the catch-words of the quack. For it is no longer a question whether these synthetic problems are to be taken up at all—it is only the question by whom: by the dispassionate mind of the scientist or by the mountebanks with their petty speculations in every sense of the word. If we open our papers and periodicals, read modern social and political novels, have a look at the mass-production of pamphlets, we find that the printing press is busy day and night in satisfying the public's wish for synthetic instruction about social affairs. Everyone knows what kind of candles are lighted there. But if unscrupulous agitators and fools exploit the public's hunger for enlightenment, the responsibility partly rests with the academic social sciences which usually refrain from even entering the ring.

It has not always been so. Academic social sciences arose in the seventeenth and eighteenth century as the synthetic science par excellence. An offspring of the post-medieval philosophy, they maintained intimate relations even to ethics and natural law far into the nineteenth century. What range of subjects was dealt with in that comprehensive science, we learn best from the life-work of Adam Smith. The most ambitious modern sociologist might be satisfied by his teaching programme. This father of economics was lecturing at Glasgow University on natural theology, ethics, national and international law, arms and "police" which is nothing else than politics comprehending economics. It is perhaps less well known that one hundred years afterwards St. W. Jevons' chair in Manchester still embraced Logic, Mental and Moral Philosophy and Political Economy.

Nevertheless in the meanwhile a fundamental transformation was in progress. On the surface it looked a natural division of labour between the various social sciences, enforced by the widening range of research. But in fact one particular branch, economics, usurped a growing preponderance. Not only were more and more special chairs for political economy established, the academic and the public interest in social problems became concentrated on the economic questions. This social superiority of economics was accompanied by a growing scientific autonomy. During the last half century the economists tried to eject just those substantial elements of their doctrines that before had linked economic research with political science, law, psychology and history—striving after "pure economics" as an independent body of exact knowledge.

One would have expected the other social sciences to have formed themselves equally as independent branches of research. But in most countries it was not so up to the last generation. There was always an academic teaching of politics but mainly connected with philosophy. The same is true of social psychology, while anthropology tended rather to the natural sciences. Finally the new science of sociology aiming at the comprehension of all our knowledge of human interrelations, could disengage itself but slowly from the philosophical and biological preconceptions of its origin. In England even to-day its academic position is not yet uncontested, and its humanist dignity is only gradually appreciated in the classical homes of study, a heavy handicap on its development, if we realize how important academic opportunities, official teaching and graduation have always been for the attractiveness and the public reputation of any particular branch of science.[1]

[1] In Germany and in the United States the social conditions and the general trend of thought during the last generation were more favourable to the development and also to the reputation of academic sociology. See Ogburn and Goldenweiser, *The Social Sciences and their Inter-Relations*, 1927, and Mannheim, *German Sociology (1918-1931)*, (*Politica*, 1934, Nr. 1, pp. 12-33). Cp. also L. von Wiese, *System der Allgemeinen Soziologie*, 1933, pp. 14-99.

CHAPTER II

THE ECONOMIC AND THE SOCIOLOGICAL ASPECT

I

How are we to understand this peculiar trend of the social sciences, the growing supremacy of economics during the nineteenth century, its striving after methodic autonomy and its lack of interest in synthetic co-operation with the kindred sciences, above all with the integrating work of modern sociology?

There are two typical answers. The first is a critical attack directed by the economist on the *substance* of sociology. Is there any need for a particular science dealing with human interrelations in general? Is there any range of problems in the field of human society which has not in the meantime been taken in hand by some specialist science like psychology, law, economics, political science and history? It is true that the definition of sociology has been for a long time a vexed question. Oscillating between an encyclopaedic research into the whole of human life and a scholastic analysis of abstract relations, it has only recently achieved a distinct delimitation of its field.[1] These difficulties of

[1] Cp. e.g. M. Ginsberg, *Sociology*, London, 1934, pp. 7-18; K. Mannheim, *Die Gegenwartsaufgaben der Soziologie*, Tübingen, 1932, pp. 6-27.

classification are connected with the fact that sociological research covers three different sets of problems.

Sociology represents in the first place a specialist science like any other section of social research, dealing with a separate topic, namely the basic forms and processes of social interrelationship generally. In this capacity it looks for the constant features in phenomena, such as contact and isolation, co-operation and struggle, equality and domination, etc., and it deals with the general types of social groups such as family, community, state, and their differences under various historical constellations. Though general sociology in this sense, because of the universality of its categories, cannot contribute much to specialist economic research, it helps to define the basic concepts of economics and to contrast them with the kindred concepts of other social sciences. Conversely general sociology uses the results of economic research as material of its own morphological work, taking e.g. the exchange process in the modern market as an extreme case of rational interrelationship which illustrates particular forms of co-operation and competition, of social ascent and decline.

The position is different with the other two fields of sociological research. These are not exclusively reserved to sociology, but require the joint effort of various social sciences. There is on the one hand the very ambitious task of synthetic sociology, which aims at analysing the structure and conditions of the process of human civilization as a whole. Starting with the working hypothesis that civilization and social order are inseparable constituents in the history of mankind, synthetic sociology examines the results of all the specialist sciences, such as law, economics, political science, art, ethics, religion, etc., from the social point of view, seeks after homogenous tendencies, and tries to determine the relative importance of the various spheres for the course of human history. For this vast work of integration sociology certainly depends on economics, and has even sometimes used the economic aspect as its main working hypothesis, as in the case of historical materialism. But one has to admit that up to the present the majority of economists on their own account have not shown much interest in the fruits of these comprehensive investigations. Though supplying their results as raw material, they are rather distrustful of the final results because of the speculative savour of such synthetic constructions in the past.

However there is on the other hand a third range of problems where sociology operates as a kind of mediator between the particular aspects of the individual social sciences. Here it investigates the concrete relations between different social factors and spheres under different circumstances. How is the legal system of a community connected with its economic structure? Do the forms of political domination influence the prevailing moral ideas? Do the religious doctrines modify economic behaviour, Max Weber's famous question? Are there even styles of thinking and of scientific research connected with the prevailing social order of different groups and times, the problem of the sociology of knowledge?

At this stage of research economics obviously cannot dispense with the collaboration of sociology, and it is not surprising that under the name of "economic sociology"[1] a kind of border-line science is developing. It tries to ascertain all social factors and influences which form and modify the "data" of the economic order and its evolution. Thus economic sociology deals on the one hand with the social institutions of the economic system, and their specific local and historical structure. How does the organization of enterprise vary in large-scale production, handicraft work, and farming? What are the differences in labour efficiency between an English and a Japanese worker? How do real wages influence the growth of population? On the other hand economic sociology is concerned with the social influences on economic behaviour, with consumers' preferences under the effect of advertisement, with the incentives of work and speculation, the motives of tariff policy or taxation. In short, all the problems we treat in applied economics, in its descriptive as well as in its political section, and in economic history, have a particular sociological aspect which requires special investigation. In

[1] For the methodic problems of economic sociology see Schumpeter, "Gustav Schmoller und die Probleme von heute" (*Schmoller's Jahrbuch*, 1926, pp. 337-88); also Bouglé, "La Sociologie Economique en France" (*Zeitschrift für Sozialforschung*, Vol. III, Nr. 3, pp. 383-408).

treating these problems economic sociology renders the general premises of economic theory concrete and gives its deductions the individual colour of space and time.

In the Western countries above all the institutionalists nowadays contribute important material to its extension, in the same manner as formerly the writers of the historical school did. Even the economic historians begin to turn more to an integration of their work with that of the economist and the sociologist—finally bringing together problems and data.[1]

II

At first sight this recent development of the relations between economics and sociology looks quite promising for the future. But closer examination shows that in economic sociology, as it is generally conceived, only the outworks of the two sciences are in contact with each other. It renders the theoretical generalizations of economics more concrete and appropriate to individual cases. But these generalizations themselves, the fundament of economic analysis, appear as an entirely independent body of knowledge, not requiring sociological research though certainly concerned with a particular section of society. In fact, the majority of modern economic theorists deny any relevance of

[1] Cp. E. Power, "On Medieval History as Social Study" (*Economica*, 1934, Nr. 1, pp. 13-29).

sociological investigations for their essential work; some of them even insist on the *a priori* character of their generalizations. In this they represent the tendency towards purification, previously mentioned, which has formalized economic theory, at least the theory of the market relations, to a degree which renders it capable of mathematical treatment. This claim is not even modern and not restricted to mathematical economics in the narrower sense, as developed by Cournot, Walras, Jevons and their followers. We can in fact discover a more general approximation to mathematical strictness of reasoning even in the classical writers, in the logical cogency of their deductions and their statements of economic "laws".

That leads us to the second reason for the unsatisfactory relation between the two sciences, this time a problem not of substance but of *method.* Justifying his reserve, the economist usually asserts that sociology can never work with the same exactness of method as economics, and that its results will never attain the same degree of certainty as his generalizations on "human behaviour in disposing of scarce means". How does this matter stand?

If we ask the outsider, what method sociology positively applies, we usually get the answer: interpretation based on inner understanding, and comparative description, but not causal analysis. We have to go back to the historical origins of modern sociology, in order to explain that popular prejudice. It is true that the inner understanding of motives plays an important role in procuring the psychological data of sociology. Further, positivism and behaviourism, especially in the United States, have brought to the forefront of a particular type of research a merely descriptive method, aiming at statistical comparisons, such as the correlation between unemployment and criminality, between social origin and fitness for military service, etc. It is also true that sympathetic understanding is a useful instrument of social research, if it is not abused metaphysically but controlled by induction, and that statistical comparisons on their part often give rise to interesting problems for further causal investigation. But this very investigation of the question how social factors typically influence each other, became the true subject of sociology, as soon as it had been constituted as an empirical science.

A statement like : " The technical concentration of the military forces and of economic production promotes the political rise of a minority dictatorship ", or the wisdom embodied in the famous slogan : " Un radical ministre n'est pas un ministre radical ", or the dispute about the influence of Calvinism on the rise of capitalism—such findings as these are not intuitional revelations at all. They are the product of a rational and empirical research, which tries to explain a chain of social interactions, every link of which is causally related to the preceding link and open to critical revision.

Once having grasped that, we must nevertheless admit that such sociological statements, though causal statements, are not demonstrated from self-evident premises. They will never attain the strictness of a mathematical generalization, but will always have to content themselves with a higher or lower degree of probability. Therefore, if it is true that the functional system of economic equilibrium or the law of supply and demand can be reduced to *a priori* axioms, sociology in comparison must certainly appear relatively nebulous.

That need not in itself diminish the scientific value of sociological research. Nobody rejects medical science in favour of say technology for the mere reason that the latter science rests on the firm ground of mathematical physics, while medicine is based on the " less exact " results of biology. The exactness of an empirical science does not consist in the formal transparency of its conclusions but in the coincidence of the rational deduction with the facts. Therefore it ultimately depends on the substance of the problems in question whether mathematical forms of thought are appropriate or not.

But it now seems that the methodic antagonism between economics and sociology displays a yet deeper divergence arising from the structure of the particular facts which form the subject of research in the two sciences. It looks as if economic theory has to deal with a reality of mathematical structure, while sociology analyses non-mathematical objects. This impression is confirmed by certain experiments which each science has made with the opposite method. Economics on the one hand attempted a non-mathematical method when the historical school invaded the field of theoretical research. The result was equally detrimental to economic science and to economic practice, and is a main cause of the modern economist's tendency to autonomy. This tendency has been reinforced by the recent attack of the institutionalists, who try once more to substitute description and probability-calculation for deductive analysis. But the true theorist feels able to deduce laws of human conduct with certainty. Therefore he declines any softening of his methodic bones and any association with sciences whose deductive schemes are less strict and less transparent.

The sociologist on the other hand is certainly striving in principle after co-operation. What nevertheless repels him is precisely the extremely rational structure of economic theory, which he feels to be a product of over-abstraction. What kind of human society is it that the economist has in mind, where human behaviour can be predicted with certainty? Does he deal with human beings at all or with mechanical atoms? The formal exactness, the approximation to mathematics, all those qualities that constitute the economist's pride, render his work suspect to a type of researcher, who is constantly faced with the mutability of human impulses, organizations and processes, and hardly ever achieves any generalization which does not need thousandfold reservations. He feels all the more justified in this critical attitude because the methodic procedure of economic theory is unique within the range of social sciences. However different problems and objects may be in social psychology, anthropology, social history, political science, there is a community of method in description and in causal interpretation in line generally with the procedure of sociology and pointing to a common idea of the structure of society.

One might perhaps try to bridge this gap by referring to the inevitable process of division of labour in modern science which presents to us one and the same object from different views and with the help of different methods. Nobody is surprised by the fact that the human body appears to the anatomist or physicist as a mechanical scaffolding, to the biologist as an organism composed out of living cells, to the psychologist as the domicile of mental qualities. However, we expect of course that all these different aspects and the methods of grasping them may be afterwards combined without logical contradiction, and may ultimately result in a higher integration of total knowledge. But the more economists and sociologists realize their particular divergencies in procedure, the more doubtful it appears to them whether their primary views can be reconciled in this way. After all they do not only deal in general with one and the same object of experience, human society, but they start also with a common setting of the problems concerning human impulses and responses, activities and relations, all of them based on the categories of general sociology. Therefore if we keep to the parallel drawn from the natural sciences, it is as though we wished to treat one part of the cellular tissue of the human body with biological methods and another part with mineralogical—the unity of the object of research has apparently been lost. It looks as if two incompatible conceptions of the primary structure of society were in rivalry. Speaking in the famous though risky analogies of the early history of the social sciences: the biological and the mechanical concept of society seem once more to rebel against each other.

At any rate we cannot help realizing that here, with the divergence of method, which obviously is more than a question of method, we touch the sore point in the actual relationship of sociology and economics. As long as we cannot explain to the sociologist, what this strange exactness of the economic laws means in social terms, how human behaviour can be described and even predicted by mathematical formula, as long as we have not demonstrated to the economist that the non-mathematical and even non-deductive statements of sociology are indispensable also for his strict conclusions, we cannot restate the case for co-operation.

III

After the foregoing considerations, we may take it for granted that the unsatisfactory state of the actual relations between economics and sociology must not be attributed to mere prejudice and lack of goodwill. Obviously a real problem is involved which touches the central substance and method of the two sciences. Following up this problem and all its implications we shall take our investigation to a stage where unbiased analysis can perhaps disclose and even conquer that apparently fundamental antagonism.

In order to go to the root of the matter we had best start with the striking features and claims of economic theory, first examining that autonomous body of economic generalizations which is said to be above any sociological implications, and the mathematical character of the economic laws. What is the meaning, the origin and the empirical bearing of these generalizations and laws, and what is their relation to the findings of sociology?

These questions are undoubtedly methodological, and they can perhaps be answered by a purely formal and axiomatic investigation. But keeping to the general rule that we test a knife by cutting rather than by whetting, we shall now leave the dry fields of methodology and advance to substantial economic analysis. Struggling with the questions of economic reality will best show us the significance and limits of the methods at issue. Of course our ultimate task remains methodological, and therefore we cannot do full justice to the economic and sociological problems which we shall use as illustrations. We shall have to cut analysis short as soon as the relation between the economic and the sociological elements in the problems under examination is cleared up, even if their substantial importance is by no means exhausted.

Now watching economics at work and paying attention to what the economists really do rather than what they contend, we shall come to most surprising conclusions. Many traditional claims and objections will appear unfounded and the fundamental antagonism fictitious. The mathematical generalizations of economic theory will themselves display a close connection with sociological ideas, but more than that : the original system of economic laws will be revealed as nothing less than a system of sociology sui generis. At the same time we shall discover that the highly rational method of economic reasoning and its striving after systematic unity and interdependence is of special importance for sociology in general, and above all for its synthetic comprehension of the social history of Western Civilization.

CHAPTER III

SIGNIFICANCE AND LIMITS OF PURE ECONOMICS[1]

I

MODERN economic theory is centred round a body of general statements, called " pure theory ". As the very name indicates, these statements are supposed to be independent of any non-economic implications. In relation to sociology, pure economics is said to be so comprehensive that its generalizations are valid for any social conditions, and therefore not to be a part of sociology, but an entirely autonomous science.

The bearing of such a claim of pure economics has been previously discussed. Closer examination will now reveal that there is something in this claim, but certainly far less than many economists contend.

The whole idea of an autonomous economic science can only arise, if there are " economic " elements in

[1] For this and the following chapter I owe many valuable suggestions to the writings of Eduard Heimann. See above all his paper on " Sociological Preconceptions of Economic Theory " (*Social Research*, vol. I, Nr. 1, pp. 22-44), but also "Sozialwissenschaft und Wirklichkeit", Tübingen, 1932, and " Soziale Theorie des Kapitalismus ", Tübingen, 1929. Cp. also H. Neisser, " Der Gegensatz von ' anschaulich ' und ' rational ' in der Geschichte der Volkswirtschaftslehre " (*Archiv. f. Sozialwissenschaft und Sozialpolitik*, vol. 65, Nr. 2, pp. 225-50) and my paper, " Über den Sinn und die Grenzen verstehender Nationalökonomie " (*Weltwirtschaftliches Archiv.*, vol. 36, Nr. 2, pp. 149-62).

human behaviour which are not necessarily " social " elements at the same time, that is to say, which do not necessarily relate to a plurality of persons, a human group. This idea is not so absurd for the economist as the outsider may think. Consider the definition of economic behaviour which we find similarly formulated in the works of scholars as far apart as Oppenheimer, Robbins, Spann : economic behaviour is concerned with disposing of scarce means for given ends. According to this definition we obviously need at least four elements, in order to constitute economic behaviour :

(1) a human subject with a plurality of ends.

(2) scarce means which can be applied in different ways (otherwise there would be no choice or disposal at all),

(3) the power of the subject in question to dispose of those means,

(4) a maxim by which the human subject arranges his means, so as to secure the satisfaction of his ends according to their relative urgency.

Now in any one of these elements social ingredients may be included which refer to group influences. The subject in question may be a human group, a family, a tribe or a nation. The means may include other people's labour and goods to be acquired by force, established tradition or exchange. The power of disposal may be lawful property, and even the scale of urgency of the wants may be determined by social influences, that is by tradition, fashion, advertisement and so on. But if social influences may operate on every datum, they need not do so. However improbable as reality, the idea of an isolated man is not logically contradictory. Why not restrict the body of means to inanimate objects? Is not the mere possession of these objects without any lawful sanction sufficient for disposal? Finally, does not the very nature of man offer him a scale of preferences, quite independent of his connection with other people? But modern economic theory as it was initiated by Jevons, Menger and Walras and was brought to its final methodic consequences by the mathematical school,[1] goes even one step further. Whether the data of its analysis, ends and means, are influenced by sociological elements or not, the decisive turn towards scientific autonomy is implied in the fact that the pure theorist does not care at all about the structure of his data. His subject does not include a critical investigation into the substance of ends, into the causes of nature's stinginess, into the scope or the constitution of the community in question. Pure theory only tries to handle a *given* body of ends and means in a particular, the "economic" way of co-ordination. What sort of way is that, and is this co-ordination of given ends and means definitely free from any sociological implications?

[1] The most extreme but thoroughly consistent conclusions from the modern approach have been drawn in H. Bernadelli, "Die Grundlagen der ökonomischen Theorie," Tübingen, 1933.

Co-ordinating scarce means to our ends according to their relative urgency, first of all impels us to form a scale of preference. We do so simply by a real or imagined act of choice, selecting a particular set of, say, food, clothing, housing facilities, etc., for each possible constellation of resources. Such an act of choice implies also a rational or irrational weighing of rival ends which bears on the various constituents of the respective sets. Still, how this selection comes about, what qualitative influences from natural or social spheres operate in that act of choice, is again of no interest for the pure theorist. He restricts his analysis to the stimuli which arise when a definite choice has been made on the basis of a given stock of means, stimuli which turn these means towards the production of the chosen set of ends.

We must not overlook the consequences of such asceticism on the part of pure economics. If we disregard the process which brings about the effectual choice, we fail to explain the ultimate forces which link just this stock of means to just this set of ends. We leave unexplained the tastes of the individuals, the origin of the means and also their distribution among the individuals. Given certain subjective desires, certain objective resources, and the social distribution of these resources, pure theory only explains the actions we usually call "production", namely (*a*) how much of the existing resources is allotted to the particular constituents of the chosen set of ends, (*b*) in what technical combinations the various resources are used.

But at the same time it is true that within these limits a supra-sociological and even mathematical side of economic behaviour becomes obvious. Right from the starting point of the individual choice, economic behaviour has a quantitative character, arranging various sets of ends in a more or less continuous series. Every member of that series is marked with a quantitative co-efficient of choice which we usually interpret as a symptom of " more or less preferredness ", even if we cannot measure the difference between these co-efficients in exact terms. As soon as a certain stock of means is given to the individual, his effectual choice within the series of sets is determined by the member with the highest co-efficient of satisfaction which can be reached under the given conditions. In the same way any change in his ends or means determines his new choice in accordance with a new series of co-efficients. Whatever the circumstances, there is always one and only one state of affairs that brings the economic disposal to rest. It may be somewhat of a metaphorical analogy to call that state of rest " subjective equilibrium ". But to apply to these actions of adjustment the condition of a maximum-minimum calculation—maximum from the viewpoint of satisfaction as a whole, minimum from the viewpoint of expenditure on each particular constituent—appears to be an adequate procedure. The strictness of these generalizations reflects only the simple fact that the individual can and does decide unambiguously in every case of economic choice, whatever his ultimate motives may be.

All these statements are elementary truisms to the modern economist. To the sociologist they reveal the ultimate reason why a supra-sociological body of strict generalizations has been established as an autonomous science of pure economics, and even with the help of mathematical terms. The quantitative character is by no means forced upon pure economics subsequently and by wrong analogy, nor has it anything to do with a " mechanical " concept of society. There is a non-sociological side of economic behaviour, in charge of the nasty business of fighting the stinginess of nature, which sets the economist the task of dealing with the colourless problems of " more " or " less ", and with that only.

In the face of this result it does not matter that every real economic action is always a part of man's social activity, and that Robinson Crusoe though logically conceivable is historically unreal. No pure theorist has ever disputed this fact. He knows that by abstracting what he holds to be the characteristic features of economic behaviour, he does not depict the whole of life. If he insists on strict distinction between economic and social attributes of man's activity, he is well aware of the fact that these abstract elements are inseparable in reality, that any economic system is embedded in a society. But the weight, expansibility, density and other physical conditions of an object also do not exist distinct from its biological attributes and its aesthetic form, and nevertheless physics could be constituted as an independent science. In the same way the stinginess of nature, a fundamental condition in man's life, appears to the modern theorist as the starting-point for a scientific cross-section. Certainly like any other branch of science, economics may afterwards apply its particular aspect to the changing meta-economic conditions of life, thus producing realistic systems of social and political economics which are appropriate to the varying constellations of economic history. But the theorist sees his true task in analysing what is common to all economic realizations, what is specifically economic in the comprehensive phenomena of the historical process, in the family order of a primitive tribe as well as in the manorial system, in capitalist society as well as in the communist state. What varies is his data, by their very variation confirming the constancy of his supra-sociological and even supra-historical generalizations.

II

Thus having grasped the meaning as well as the universal validity of pure economics, we still may ask what range of problems is explained by its statements. We cannot test its importance except by studying its bearing on some concrete economic questions. Above all we are to examine whether the gist of its supra-sociological generalizations, the theory of choice and of subjective equilibrium, really leads into the centre of economic activity under any social conditions whatsoever, and whether social attitudes and institutions are in fact nothing but changeable data of autonomous economic transactions.

Reviewing the historical realizations of economic activity, we will keep to the traditional classification of centralized and decentralized systems, using the social order of the disposal of means as the fundamental distinction. This point of view has the great advantage of bringing into prominence the particular characteristics that distinguish modern Western economy from all other economic organizations in history: free exchange versus authoritarian regulation.

The various authoritarian systems largely confirm the principal statements of pure theory. Whether they are based on family order or on national public property, on democratic equality or on hierarchical disparity, there is always a central authority which functions as the economic subject. By " evaluating the importance of the members and their desires for the life of the group " (Heimann), it forms the general scale of preference according to the prevailing social ideas. Thus it prepares the social order of distribution as a datum for the only economic activity that is left: the adequate allotment of the means.

In a decentralized system of free exchange the institutional data of economic behaviour are certainly qualified in a particular way. There must be at least two economic subjects both of them disposing of some means and allowing each other's claim to do so. Exchange is added to seizure and labour as a method of allocating the available means. But these new facts apparently have only a meta-economic significance, determining the frame but not the substance of this kind of economic organization. The ultimate criterion as to economic behaviour still seems to be the act of choice of the partners in exchange according to their respective scales of preference, each aiming at the maximum subjective satisfaction. Though they cannot attain any satisfaction at all except by means of a compromise in bargaining, the action of exchange marks the point in both of their scales, which gives each of them the maximum of satisfaction under existing conditions. Apparently in this way exchange and market system do not only confirm, but even extend the general theory of choice. It is the real triumph of the theory of exchange that its statements pass beyond the rather vague conception of a mere subjective equilibrium. Exchanging certain measurable quantities of goods, the partners are able to determine the optimum point of mutual satisfaction in terms of computable magnitudes, thus giving the original quantitative disposition of economic behaviour an objective expression. It is now only a small step to the formulation of the law of supply and demand, the general form of our various rules and generalizations in exchange theory; the pure deduction of the theory of prices and income, of market equilibrium and its variations seems to be completed without any reference to sociological conditions.

Here we enter the realm of the economic laws which have established the traditional reputation of economics. By dealing with external exchange relations instead of internal valuations, these laws of the market claim not only universal validity for every bargaining transaction, but also mathematical exactness in the sense of calculability. They seem to suggest that we can strictly deduce bargaining behaviour without caring at all about its ends and motives, and determine the movement of prices, even if every buyer and seller has free choice of action. So striking a result which at the same time contradicts the sociologist's general experience calls for closer examination.

III

The substance of such a price law becomes manifest if we take the simplest form of the law of supply and demand. " When, at the price ruling demand exceeds supply, the price tends to rise." Or, if we prefer a less mechanical but more comprehensive language : If the buyers increase the total demand for a commodity, other things remaining equal, the sellers will in the first place raise their sale prices.

Will they really ? According to our daily experience we are inclined to answer that it is fairly probable that they will. But the statements of the general theory of choice with which we were dealing till now did not restrict their validity to mere probability; those deductive generalizations claimed the character of certainty. Unfortunately we cannot guarantee such certainty in respect of the sellers' behaviour. There may be a pupil of Tolstoi or Gandhi among them, declining such an "exploitation" of the buyers, or a native of the Trobriand Islands, whose inhabitants are famous for working for the sake of work itself and for giving away three-quarters of their product for nothing. What shall we do with these cases?

At first sight these exceptions do not weaken the position of the pure theorist. Far from disregarding such possibilities, he includes them within his categories of subjective equilibrium. Whether I am interested chiefly in profit or in sacrifice, in my own or in other people's advantage, when dealing in the market I shall always find among the given opportunities one position of optimum exchange that will bring my transactions to rest. That is certainly true. Nevertheless we cannot help realizing that such an interpretation of equilibrium and of variation of prices is not quite in harmony with the far-reaching conclusions usually drawn from the law of demand and supply, and that this interpretation is certainly not very "exact". It will not allow any spectator of the market process, either theorist or business man, to make any previous calculation about the effective price relations and their reaction to changes in demand. All he can say is that, whatever will happen, in the end there will be another state of equilibrium, the prices being either higher or lower or equal, the volumes of transactions being greater or smaller or unchanged.

This and only this can be deduced by "pure" reasoning, that is to say, as long as we keep to the assumption that every partner in the market, the seller no less than the buyer, is entirely free in his choice of action. If the classical writers and their modern followers, and above all the normal business men, state objective rules of behaviour, and if they deduce determinate variations of prices from changes in demand, they overstep the boundaries of pure theory. It may be true that maximum prices reduce production, that free trade stimulates exports, that wage-cuts increase employment, but it does not follow from pure reasoning. That follows only if we restrict the absolute freedom of choice, and prescribe a determinate behaviour at least to the sellers, as in fact the classical writers did.

It is well known that it is the conception of the *economic man* which has provided the basis of all exact laws of the market from the classical age to this day. If for the moment we disregard all his hedonist features, the economic man expresses a very formal maxim of behaviour. This maxim has no concern with the ultimate ends and motives of the economic actions, be they egoistic or altruistic, Benthamist or Gandhist, because it is not related to the use of the outcome of any bargain, but to behaviour *in* bargaining. It postulates that in buying and selling we prefer the larger advantage to the smaller one, calculated not in subjective return of pleasure but in objective quantities of goods or money. "The buyer to the cheapest market, the seller to the dearest," is the economic man's motto.

Only if we insert this working rule into the general categories of pure reasoning, do the price laws acquire a substantial and even exact content. In other words, only if we postulate a certain rule of conduct in bargaining, do the movements of the exchange economy become calculable for the spectator and, what is even more important, for the members of the system themselves.[1] After all, it need not be just the maxim of the economic man that renders price laws and market variations determinate, though we have not experienced any other maxim in the historical systems of free exchange. In theory, any substantial rule of bargaining conduct fixes the process of exchange in definite lines, and suggests to every member how to call forth from his partner behaviour which meets his own wants. But whatever maxim we choose, it cannot be deduced from pure economics. It must be produced from the realm of social psychology, bringing an unquestionably sociological element into the pure theory of the market. And it does not come in as one of the numerous border-line data which give the analysis the individual colour of space and time, confirming

[1] See P. A. Rosenstein, "The Rôle of Time in Economic Theory" (*Economica*, 1934, Nr. 1, pp. 93, 94) for the demonstration that a postulate is hidden in the spuriously analytical equations of the mathematical theory of the market.

rather than transforming the generalizations of pure economics. By restricting one of the categories of pure reasoning, namely freedom of choice on the side of the economic subjects, sociology enters into the centre of the theory of the exchange system.[1]

IV

Sociology intrudes, however, at yet another point. In its classical formulation and even in its everyday meaning, the law of supply and demand further indicates that generally that price tends to be reached at which supply and demand are equal. At first sight we might interpret even this assertion in a " pure " sense, indicating that wherever a bargain takes place, the point of equilibrium between subjective expenditure and subjective return will be attained for both partners. But again such a statement is not very exact. Therefore the idea of the equation of supply and demand is mainly interpreted in a much narrower and more concrete sense. It now points to the tendency of the market system to effect only one price for the same commodity at the same moment which is equal to the

[1] J. S. Mill has applied the conception of " middle principles " to such sociological elements which constitute " uniformities of co-existence between the states of the various social phenomena " because " not every variety of combination of these general social facts is possible, but only certain combinations " (*Logic*, Book VI, Chapter X, §§2 and 6). In his *Sociology*, London, 1934, Professor Ginsberg has revived this methodological idea which is a particularly useful instrument for grasping structural connections in social research. See also Karl Mannheim, *Mensch und Gesellschaft im Zeitalter des Umbaus*, Leiden, 1935, pp. 125-49.

money costs of its production, and therefore to equalize money returns for all sellers of the same commodity. In this way the vague conception of a mere subjective equilibrium between expenditure and return of pleasure is rendered concrete and extended to an objective equilibrium of computable magnitudes such as money costs and money returns.

Behind the " exactness " of the law of supply and demand in this interpretation, in addition to the bargaining principle of the economic man, another meta-economic assumption is hidden. If the sellers react to increased demand by raising their prices above costs, at first they distort objective equilibrium, and the quantitative relations in the particular section of the market again become incalculable. The maxim of the economic man as such determines only the direction of the market variations, but not, as we see, the new point of rest. This point is defined, only if the sellers answer rising prices by increasing supply, and thus restore equality between prices and costs or, in other words, if the market system provides a particular device which induces the sellers to react not merely in the sphere of pricing but also in that of producing.

This time the matter in question is no psychological maxim but an objective social institution: viz. *competition*. Perfect competition means that the bargaining partners are not isolated dealers, not " monopolists " in the literal sense of the word, but that on both sides many other members of the market join in the bargaining struggle. This situation compels every individual to defend his bargaining position in two directions : against the contracting party opposite and against the competing party alongside. The economic man's behaviour is at one and the same time restricted and stimulated, restricted with regard to the process of pricing, stimulated with regard to the process of production. By the market transactions thus set in motion, all deviations from the calculable state of rest are turned into short run frictions, and the recurrent intervals of objective disequilibrium and incalculability are reduced to negligible magnitudes. The whole meaning of the term " objective " in respect of equilibrium and disequilibrium becomes manifest at the same time. Prices, changes in prices and the relation between prices and costs do not only represent computable magnitudes ; in a perfect market they face the individual bargaining partner as objective data which he cannot manipulate, but to which he has to conform.

But with that we have taken another far-reaching step into sociology. Perfect competition prevails only if all members of the system are *willing* and *able* to react promptly to any changes in the market constellation. Their *willingness* is secured as soon as the maxim of the economic man is adopted ; but on what preconditions does their *ability* depend ?

There are in the first place some political conditions. They relate to the lawful right of every individual freely to dispose of his means. Not only must his private property as such be guaranteed ; in addition to that there must not be any monopolization of means either imposed or contracted, an assumption we usually include in the conception of "free exchange". Such evidence by definition does not apply to a technical condition of ability to compete which is no less important. It is here not so much a question of natural monopolies, as of the technical state produced by social organization. With equal natural resources the opportunity to compete is quite different according as industrially the large-scale production system or the small-scale handicraft system prevails. A relatively high proportion of capital, within the totality of applied means, or a high degree of specialization of labour renders the producers' reaction to changes in prices much more difficult than a general prevalence of high ratios of unskilled labour does.[1] The long-lasting effects of sunk costs check the mobility of the economic subjects as well as of the means. Since money costs and prices cannot be adjusted in the short run, deviation from objective equilibrium persists under such technical conditions, and the market relations become incalculable.

We had to admit that the validity of the exact market laws depends on a definite psychological condition. Now we have to realize that this validity is actually confined to a very limited political and technical state of affairs.

[1] Cp. for all details, J. M. Clark, *The Economics of Overhead Costs*, Chicago, 1923, a true gold-mine also for the sociologist.

CHAPTER IV

THE "SOCIETY OF EXCHANGE"

I

We have discovered two sociological principles underlying as logical conditions the exact laws of the market: the economic man on the one hand, competition or mobility of the productive factors on the other hand. Very formless as we dug them out of the quantitative relations of exchange, they take on colour and shape in the sociologist's hand. He discovers in these plain data no disparate social elements, but a coherent system of society. Reflecting on economic man he meets the human type of Western civilization during the liberal age: active and rational, independent of the political, legal and religious bonds of earlier times, but also lacking the earlier individuality of spacial and temporal form, representing a social atom within a large body of homogeneous elements, a body linked together not by a central order, by irrational sentiments or tradition, but by an immense tissue of individual bargaining transactions. Civil liberty, private property rights, free decision of the individual as to his bargaining, at the same time a structure of the material equipment that does not prevent shifting, whenever a change in the market conditions suggests a change in business and work—a concrete idea of social psychology, of the political and legal constitution is combined with a definite conception of technique: small-scale organization of many independent producers. Far from presenting a pure theory appropriate to any social conditions, so simple a law as the law of supply and demand, as soon as we take it in its exact meaning, depicts the essential features of a very concrete society: the liberal society of early capitalism.

For this reason it is not at all surprising that it was the classical writers who first formulated the laws of the market in their exact form. It is the fundamental structure of their contemporary economy which they wanted to describe with the help of a particular bargaining rule and of objective equilibrium. But closer examination will show us that it was more than a historical accident when free exchange as an economic system was propagated in just this constellation. The particular preconditions which give rise to the exact laws of the market are themselves of profound sociological significance.

II

No doubt the sociological middle principles as assumed in the classical theory of the market are not the necessary background of every real bargaining transaction. Quite apart from the somewhat far-fetched psychological examples I referred to, there are manifold occasional exchange actions in every primitive society which often take place under the strangest conditions. But also every fully developed exchange system shows us many transactions where the bargaining vigour of buyers or sellers and the efficacy of competition on one or both sides is checked by numerous subjective and objective factors. The watch-word " Buy British Goods ! " contradicts the economic man's motto in the same way as the boycott of Jewish shops, and though the rule applies to factors of production no less than to commodities, a rise of the rate of interest does not always stimulate saving and a fall of wages certainly not always reduce supply of labour.

The theoretical explanation which all these transactions need can be offered by pure theory, as long as the concrete scales of preference of the respective partners are *given* from any sources whatsoever. But the practical value of this statement is very small, because the individual demand-curves are hardly ever given or to be procured. However, even if we could thus analyse some isolated actions of exchange, we can never in this way explain the functioning of exchange as the general order of an economic *system*, not merely because we lack necessary information, but for fundamental objective reasons.

As soon as the satisfaction of wants entirely depends on exchange relations, the individuals cannot rely any longer on the vague notion that their own actions will be answered by their bargaining partners in some way or other. For the sake of their ultimate satisfaction they must be sure that a definite rule of conduct will be observed generally. The market system can persist as general and permanent economic organization only if the impulses of every member as to quantity and quality of production, expressed by his price offers, are reacted to in a determinate manner. Otherwise in spite of division of labour, the individual is worse off in such a system than in Robinson Crusoe's state of isolation. Though badly equipped in comparison with a member of an exchange economy, Crusoe at least knows that he will get what he may require under the existing order of means, because he depends only on himself. But the member of an exchange economy can make use of his large virtual opportunities only if his bargaining partners behave as economic men and react to higher price offers by increasing supply. It is the very paradox of an exchange system that having to deal with Gandhi's moral disciples endangers my life, while partners who use me as a means to their enrichment will ultimately grant me all the advantages of a large market. This finding is already hidden in Adam Smith's famous sentence: "It is not from the benevolence of the butcher . . . that we expect our dinner, but from his regard to his own interest." But it is certainly not implied in the supra-sociological generalizations of pure theory. In the best possible case they give snapshots of independent durationless cross-sections of the market, but never a film of the exchange process through time, that is to say, of the market as the basic structure of an economic system.[1]

One might perhaps say that this restriction is not particularly characteristic of an exchange system, that also in an authoritarian order the future of the system must be determined by special devices. But this very consideration brings to light the full difference in the bearing of pure reasoning on the two systems. In an authoritarian economy the decision on the economic process through time, that is to say, on the persistence of the group and its members, is a part of the total decision of the central authority, embodied in its scale of preference. In an exchange system the individual's arbitrary scale of preference as such does not necessarily include a maxim that brings the economic process through time into harmony with the wants of his partners. The competence of the central authority having been cancelled, the members themselves have to make up for the usurpation of autonomy by voluntarily restricting their freedom of action. Exchange cannot be efficient and cannot even continue as a basic form of an economic system, unless the permanent interrelationship between the partners is secured and substantially guided by a substitute authority implied in a general working rule of bargaining behaviour.

It is just the same with the principle of competition. Neither objective equilibrium nor perfect

[1] See Schumpeter, *Das Wesen und der Hauptinhalt der theoretischen Nationalökonomie*, Leipzig, 1908, pp. 443-77, and recently Bernadelli, op. cit., p. 78, n.3.

competition are necessary conditions of any isolated exchange transaction. The theory of imperfect competition[1] which disregards that principle certainly deals with practical situations and may even gain a growing importance in the face of increasing monopolization. But it is not the causes of imperfection, but the still operating forces of competition which have till now maintained exchange as the structural element of the modern economic system. The theory of imperfect competition stresses the destructive rather than the constructive features of the real exchange order. By the same degree as it is more general and more "pure" than the classical conception of the law of supply and demand, it is less "exact" and less useful for disclosing the fundamental structure of the market.

III

Economic man and competition as basic conditions of such a "society of exchange" secure efficiency and continuance of production. However, the market can function as an economic system, only if not merely the buyers' impulses are safely transmitted

[1] The conception of imperfect competition as recently expounded by Mr. Chamberlin and Mrs. Robinson even includes the cases above referred to as exceptions of the economic man's conduct. In order not to darken my reasoning by a terminology which is certainly illuminating for many special problems of economic analysis but still uncommon and even strange to the sociological mode of thinking, I keep to the traditional identification of imperfect competition with any kind of monopoly including immobility for technical reasons, that is, with any long run deviation from objective equilibrium which is caused by "objective" factors.

to the sellers' productive activity, but if also these impulses themselves are permanently kept working by continuous provision of purchasing power. In other words, the exchange system has to settle not only production, but also social distribution.

Pure theory, as we have seen, regards distribution as a *datum* of economic disposal, a view which the structure of an authoritarian system rather confirms. There the social order determining the allocation of the available means to the members forms a part of the authority's general scale of preference, and is in fact an outside datum of the productive process which in principle requires to be confirmed afresh in every period of production. The exchange system does not possess any special organ of this kind. It is the social preconditions of its order of production which are also to secure the order of social distribution. Striving after the maximum of money return does not only determine prices and quantities of commodities but also prices and volumes of the agents of production. Perfect competition equalizes the prices and the average costs of goods, but at the same time equalizes the incomes and the marginal productivity of the agents. It is one and the same operation looked at from two sides. But only the twofold relation constitutes exchange as an autonomous process. There is a continuous chain of mutual causation at work by which the result of production, that is the incomes, of one period determines the capacity of consumption, that is demand, of the following period, this effectual demand on its part determining the future incomes and so forth.

The statement of pure theory that social distribution and incomes are data of the bargaining transactions is not logically wrong, but it is again based on a fundamentally durationless view of the market. For the market as a process through time social distribution is an outside datum only in the very beginning, constituted by the original order of property rights. Once the exchange process is started, we cannot, looking at its course, any longer distinguish between data and results, as far as production and distribution, prices and incomes are concerned. The autonomous circular flow (Kreislauf) of the market constantly reproduces the constellation for a new start.

Perhaps one might ask whether the chain of the market relations depends on the combined efficacy of both the social factors, or whether the principle of the economic man does not suffice to reproduce the circular flow even under imperfect competition. Certainly incomes and future demand arise from monopoly prices just as well as from competitive prices. But on the one hand we can exactly calculate the relations between the demand for a product and the incomes of the agents engaged in its production, only if money costs coincide with prices. On the other hand, and this is even more important, every imperfection of competition necessarily starts a process of social redistribution in the sense of a transformation of the relative shares in the total purchasing power. It depends on the extent and the application of the monopolistic profits, whether this deflection from objective equilibrium endangers the continuance of the system. At any rate as in the sphere of production, monopolization brings forces into operation also in the sphere of distribution which in the long run distort rather than reinforce steadiness. In that way the classical idea that the conditions of calculability of the market are identical with the conditions of stability is once more confirmed.

IV

The identification of the perfect market with the stable market implies yet another far-reaching sociological assumption. If the system is to be maintained through time, the autonomous forces of exchange have to secure a minimum income for every partner just as the leader of an authoritarian economy has to grant his subjects a minimum allocation of means. Therefore the original distribution of property and incomes has either to provide a satisfactory share for every member which is simply to be reproduced by the exchange process, or any unsatisfactory start is to be corrected afterwards by the autonomous evolution of the circular flow. Thus the theory of the exchange system necessarily includes also a statement as to the origin and even as to the evolution of the market conditions.

Now the original order of social distribution certainly is a true datum of any exchange process. For every real market system this order is an historical fact that cannot be deduced by general reasoning, but is to be found out by empirical research. It is not permissible simply to assume that the original distribution was equal or at least tolerable for all, even if history did not show the contrary on every page. Therefore, some of the classical writers did well to try it the other way round, seeking rather to demonstrate that whatever the social start, the very functioning of the market initiates a general evolution which tends to establish a more and more satisfactory order for all members.

It is this aiming at a strict deduction also of economic evolution which gives an important systematic place within the classical analysis to such peculiar hypotheses as the law of population, the iron law of wages, the conception of the saving process, etc. All these ideas serve only one purpose, namely to extend the range of determinateness and calculability to the sphere of the natural and social data of the market process, and thus to facilitate an estimate of the direction and limits of possible dynamic changes of the system as a whole. It is not only distribution which has been deprived of the character of an independent datum within the continuous process of exchange. Even the other objective conditions of the system, the growth of population, the accumulation of means and the technique of production are now involved in the same process. By stating a dependence of the birth-rate on the wage-level, of the wage-level on saving, of saving on profits, of profits on technical progress, of technical progress on improving division of labour, of this improvement on extension of markets, that is, of the scope of the society of exchange, already Adam Smith completed the internal chain between the productive and the distributive process of the market by an external chain of mutual dependence between the natural and social data of its circular flow. The unbreakable circle or rather spiral line of the total evolution protects the individual bargaining transactions against unaccountable distortions from outside. By allowing only small and slow changes, this evolutionary order of the data finally guarantees the persistence of objective equilibrium between prices and costs, money expenditure and money returns, and definitely reduces any deviations to mere short run frictions.

At the same time the trend of general evolution appeared to Adam Smith and his closer adherents as necessarily favourable for all classes of exchange partners. Progressive division of labour was taken as permanently increasing real return. But what is even more important from the point of view of distribution, by stimulating accumulation of money capital the same technical progress was constantly to raise the wage-level. In this way the autonomous forces of the market were ultimately to indemnify those classes which came off badly in the early stages.

Now we realize how manifold and complicated the logical modalities of the concept of objective equilibrium are, and also the sociological structure described by this concept. It assumes not only a definite order of the individual exchange action, but also of the total process of economic evolution. However, closer examination reveals that it is still the same basic factors which condition both. If the birth-rate is to follow the movements of the wage-level and the saving-rate the changes in profits, obviously economic man is supposed to operate in the market of the factors of production as he does in the commodity market. If rising profits stimulate accumulation and investment, apparently competition tends to adjust the scope of production to the alterations of productivity. The law of general evolution is based on social and technical mobility just as the law of supply and demand is, when applied to the individual bargaining transactions. Finally, the main condition of technical mobility, "labour intensive" small-scale production, is also the foundation of the optimistic prognosis which connects freedom of exchange with social justice and thus with general economic efficiency and stability. Only so long as accumulation of capital immediately increases demand for labour, does technical progress benefit all classes in production as in consumption, and gradually reduce the social advantages which have been inherited by the propertied classes.

V

The economic theorist often prides himself on the fact that his generalizations have something of the strictness and calculability of a natural law. In the course of our analysis it gradually occurred to us that this claim is justified only under very special sociological conditions. But these conditions once assumed, the statement implies more than a metaphorical analogy. It gives adequate expression to the fact that free exchange secures the permanent satisfaction of a group, only if the individual bargaining transaction as well as the general trend of evolution take place in a regular form. And it is not a question of this or that type of regularity, but of being fixed on the lines which are described by the domination of the economic man and of perfect competition in every sphere of social life, from breeding of human beings through saving of material means up to buying and selling of commodities and services.

In speaking of natural laws of the market, the classical writers referred not only to the strictness of the linkage but also to the structural essence of society they thought embodied in these concatenations. We may leave this philosophical speculation of a rationalist age where it is, and need not discuss the question whether the World Spirit has intended free exchange to be the ultimate solution of man's economic and social troubles. But if for whatever reasons society is to be based on the market order, it is true that only the exceptional constellation which the classical writers explicitly or implicitly assumed secures its proper functioning. It was this interest in structural analysis which produced the strange mixture of realistic inquiries and utopian postulates in the classical doctrines. In constructing their systems, these writers did not trouble about all the individual features of their economic age, but only about those real forces which they thought beneficial for the development and consolidation of a system of free association.

One might perhaps object that fixing social behaviour and technical order once for all on rigid lines absolutely contradicts the idea of personal spontaneity and freedom. The paradoxical answer is that a certain kind of depersonalization is the price of economic and political freedom. A system which casts off centralized regulation has to make up for the loss of external order by subjecting its members to internal rules of self-restriction.[1] By standardizing market conduct and social and technical institutions, the classical writers certainly effaced the boundaries between man's spontaneity and nature's determinateness. Thus they positively gave rise to an idea of society which bears some resemblance to the mechanical conceptions of the natural sciences. One might even say that a trace of materialist interpretation of history lurks in this theory. It tries after all

[1] That even the economic man is to behave within the bounds of "justice" and "self-command", follows from Adam Smith's *Theory of Moral Sentiments*.

to explain the structure of social order generally by the laws of that sphere which on account of human wants is essentially concerned with nature including man as a factor of production. But from whatever philosophical speculations this idea may once have sprung, it implies a true finding as to the order of a society of free association to be built and preserved between authority and anarchy. And it definitely reveals sociology of the largely depersonalized order of a liberal Utopia to be the ultimate meaning of the exact laws of classical economics.

VI

Summarizing our results we may say :

(*a*) There are on the one hand some supra-sociological generalizations of pure theory. They are valid for any economic disposal but they are not calculable in objective magnitudes.

(*b*) There are on the other hand some exact laws of exchange. They are calculable in objective magnitudes but they are valid for only one special order of the market, based on a particular constellation of sociological elements.

(*c*) Embodied in the exact laws of exchange, these sociological elements certainly do not present themselves in the qualitative shape in which social reality brings them to life. They appear in the form of quantitative relations between economic elements, that is to say, as co-existence and sequence, rest and motion, shifting and readjustment, maximum and minimum, more or less of prices and volumes. This transformation of the qualitative richness of social reality into the bare concepts of the economic man and competition brings the original and perpetual mathematical disposition of economic behaviour to light.

(*d*) But exactness and calculability of the market relations are not to be attributed to the pure essence of economic behaviour, but exclusively to the introduction of these sociological middle principles into the pure theory of exchange. In contradistinction to other data which make analysis merely specific, these elements do not only give nuances of space and time to combinations which were already exact in themselves. It is the insertion of these socio-historical constituents into the perpetual categories of exchange and nothing else which transforms the vague and almost tautological idea of subjective equilibrium into a strict system of objective relations and calculable variations.

(*e*) Therefore the exact laws of the market have no deductive self-evidence at all but the mere probability which marks every empirical law. The degree of probability of their realization depends upon how probable it is that the basic social conditions will themselves materialize, that is to say, on the historical fact whether and to what extent liberal society exists.

CHAPTER V

THE SOCIOLOGICAL FACTOR IN MODERN ECONOMIC THEORY

I

OUR considerations relating to a society of exchange have also disclosed the real foundations of the academic and practical preponderance of economics within the social sciences during the nineteenth century. This preponderance and, linked up with it, the claim of economic theory to autonomy of method corresponds to a social reality which was to assume the form of economic interrelationship. Certainly this kind of autonomy means the very contrary of suprasociological purity. Ultimately it points to no mere question of procedure but to the substantial facts of a definite social reality, or at least of the historical tendencies making for the materialization of such a reality, namely to the cogency of a self-acting circular flow of bargaining transactions. In the interpretation of this unique state of affairs economic and sociological analysis necessarily become one and the same thing.

The early classical writers, above all Adam Smith, were well aware of that twofold aspect of their investigations.[1] For them liberal society was still a postulate, and analysis was one of the weapons in

[1] Cp. Ingram, *A History of Political Economy*, Edinburgh, 1888, pp. 87-93.

the struggle for its realization. But the more the social life of the nineteenth century adopted some outward forms of the classical utopia, the more did methodic awareness diminish among their followers. Soon after Ricardo the idea arose that it is exchange order as such, irrespective of its particular social and technical environment, which makes for productivity as well as for stability in an autonomous circular flow. Perhaps one could have dispensed with profounder insight if social reality had not fundamentally changed. To be quite accurate, it was not so much a change which the social trend underwent during the rise of the industrial system, as a line of evolution entirely different from the prognostications of the classical writers, though some of their political and psychological postulates have been realized.

It is not within the range of this study to describe the economic and social transformation during the industrial age. But we can descry the essential features simply by going back to the general categories of economic behaviour and by reflecting on their peculiar stamp in modern times. The economic subjects, far from remaining homogeneous atoms, have linked themselves by new forms of large-scale organization and bargaining associations into widely differing social molecules. The order of means is characterized by a new type of capital-requiring and labour-saving technique whose dynamics effects complicated forms of substitution among the agents of production, discontinuous processes of adjustment and above all a growing immobilization of the forces of the market. The order of distribution shows no tendency at all towards equality but rather a plutocratic turn under the redistributive influence of the exchange process itself. And even the economic incentive has lost something of its classical distinctness. It is not exactly Gandhism and Trobriandism that more and more rivals Benthamism, but national, social and racial canons of behaviour which obscure the simple principle of money incentive. The ultimate result of all these transformations is the very opposite of the classical state of objective equilibrium; the deviations have become larger and longer-lasting, the readjustments slow and incomplete; the circular chain breaks periodically. Economic behaviour has ceased to be the model of perfect social interaction.

II

How has modern economics mastered this very unclassical world? How did it accommodate the simple exactness of the classical market laws to the complicated network of industrial dynamics? What has become of the spurious autonomy of realistic exchange theory, and of the frictionless unity of economic and sociological research?

This essay is not concerned with the history of economic doctrines, though a critical survey of these doctrines from the point of view of their sociological implications might well complete the existing systematic treatises. Such a survey would have to describe on the one hand an obstinate lack of realism among the dogmatic followers of the classical writers, on the other hand a long series of more or less revolutionary transformations of the classical system, starting about a century ago when French sociologists and German historians initiated a process of self-criticism. Though this process afterwards degenerated into the misconstructions of the "Methodenstreit", its ultimate motives have not lost topical interest. We shall meet the lasting results of that discussion, if we now examine the position of modern realistic theory and its relations to sociology.

The main methodic ideas as to the analysis of the modern industrial system can be arranged in five groups :

(1) There are first of all the traditional post-classical writers. Protesting against the new reality rather than explaining it, they keep to the sociological preconceptions of the classical system to this day, even if they have abandoned most of its special doctrines. They believe in mobility and objective equilibrium as the true and permanent essence not only of the ideal but also of the real market process, an essence that, in their opinion, has been obscured and perverted by influences arising exclusively from the non-economic aspects of society.

(2) Refusing any modification of the classical assumptions these epigoni provoked the passionate opposition of the historical and institutional schools against any form of deductive theory. We are

indebted to these empirical researchers for the creation of " economic sociology " in the descriptive meaning of the concept, that is, for enriching our knowledge with new facts and concrete data. But the surrender of analysis and the reduction of economic research generally to mere description, means not the reform but the abolition of theory.

(3) Tired of this methodic confusion, the schools of Vienna and Lausanne tried to turn all historical assumptions out of economic theory, and gradually established that body of pure generalizations we referred to above. It is obvious that the pure theorist as such cannot contribute much to the illumination of a concrete economic system like modern industrialism. All he may properly deduce from his categories is, as we have seen, the durationless subjective equilibrium, a snapshot of individual positions in which the continuity of objective processes is lost.

Certainly the pure theorist is not always consistent. By unconsciously introducing some socio-historical specifications, he sometimes falls into the lower stage of abstraction which corresponds to the classical reasoning. This overstepping of the methodic bounds usually happens as soon as the analysis of choice and value proceeds to a theory of prices. But even if he intentionally moves within the realistic sphere, the pure theorist hardly ever advances to analysing the main structure of the various historical manifestations of the exchange order. In principle he prefers instrumentalistic reasoning on possible individual constellations to outlining the general ground-plan and the basic forces of an economic "system". If he speaks in terms of a system at all, he usually thinks of the logical arrangement of our analytical tools and of the unity of our machinery for the solution of problems (Schumpeter) rather than of the substantial reproduction of any historical reality. He does not recognize any useful findings intermediate between the universal categories and the individual phenomena of the economic world. And if he is blamed for disregarding the realm of the "middle principles" and of the "realistic system" in the sense of a structural analysis of various economic periods, the pure economist cites the natural scientist whose investigations, he claims, are equally restricted to the universal law on the one hand and to the individual case on the other hand.[1]

[1] Though very popular in modern methodological discussions this analogy misguidedly identifies the universal laws of the natural sciences with the categories of pure economics. In contradistinction to the statements of pure theory, e.g. the law of gravitation does not consist in the vague notion that some relation always exists between the time during which a body falls and the distance through which it falls. This statement became a natural law only when a *constant value* was discovered which rendered the relation calculable under any circumstances. Beyond that, knowledge of the particular conditions of the individual case is only needed, because there are always external influences deflecting the *concrete* value of the constant from the *ideal* value, for which allowances are to be made. But even if these corrections are not possible in every practical case, in principle the ideal value of the constant is confirmed as the average value of sufficient "pure" observations.

In economics, empirical constants of this kind have not yet been discovered though investigations were made as far back as 250 years ago, e.g. by Gregory King. Recently the work of realistic theorists

(4) The pure theorist with his methodological radicalism is rather a novelty in Anglo-Saxon economics. There the typical approach to our problem is represented by Marshall. He rather disliked the higher stages of abstraction, and generally kept to the intermediate sphere of classical deduction, with good reason calling himself a pupil of Ricardo. He was, of course—and that distinguishes him from the epigoni—too much of an expert in the real affairs of economy and society simply to rattle off the classical preconceptions. But he did not fundamentally alter the systematic position of the economic man or of competition. He modified these concepts step by step, whenever the flow of his analysis required re-shaping and completion. Therefore his writings are full of the finest instrumentalistic investigations into special problems, and there is nobody in the scientific world of economics during the last two generations who has contributed equally to the refinement of our analytical tools. That this very procedure is sometimes a stumbling-block for the essentially systematic mind, shows only the black side of his particular virtues. Maintaining in

---

and statisticians has turned to systematic research on the possibility of statistical laws of supply and demand. Only if these attempts of Pigou, Moore, Frisch, Schultz, Leontief, Marschak and others should prove successful, economics will possibly take on the methodic character of the natural sciences. In the meantime we might well use an advantage the social sciences have over the natural sciences, namely to discover some of the constants of the modern market system by the refinement of what Marshall has called "qualitative analysis". Cp. below, pp. 101, 139-45.

principle the classical framework but widening and refining it, his miniature-realism has almost achieved by putting the new wine into old bottles what the historical school has aspired to in vain: the construction of a totality out of perfectly analysed particles.

At that point certainly we touch the limits of his procedure. He resembles the pre-Copernican astronomers. As a matter of fact they solved many problems of their age, but only with the help of very complicated auxiliary constructions, thus obscuring the structure of the whole by keeping to obsolete principles. Now is there any Copernicus in the field of realistic theory?

(5) We are used to contemplating the analytical work of the last two generations from the point of view of the theory of value, and we tend to emphasize the subjective turn in all modern investigations. It is this line of thought which has produced pure economics on the one hand and the mathematical treatment of partial and general equilibria on the other hand. But at the same time in the realm of realistic theory a methodic transformation has been initiated, the results of which will perhaps prove even more important for the future position of economics as a social science.

The true originator of this evolution was Marx. I am not thinking either of his socialism or his Hegelianism or his historical materialism or even his theory of labour value. His great systematic achievement was the discovery that large-scale organization and permanent technical progress determine the structure and dynamics of the capitalist market process. On this basis he recast the classical system by supplanting some of its sociological middle principles by others. Thus he took up once more the investigation into the essential conditions of the market as an economic system and into its progressive tendencies. From the methodological point of view it does not matter whether Marx always proceeded correctly in detail. What makes him a pioneer is his idea of constructing another economic theory of circular flow and evolution at the same level of abstraction as the classical writers, but on substantially different assumptions, and the conscious tenacity of his hold on the sociological implications of his economic theory.

Marx' methodic procedure has found various followers during the last generation, and within all schools of economic thought. If we take writers so diametrically opposed in their substantial ideas as Wicksell, Oppenheimer, Schumpeter and J. M. Clark, we find them agreed on one general principle. In their realistic systems they do not confine themselves to instrumentalistic reasoning on hypothetical constellations. All of them reconsider the circular process of the market as a whole on the assumption that one or more non-classical elements dominate the social order : banking organization or flight from the land, a dynamic type of economic man or the cost conditions of large-scale production.

III

The great methodological progress accomplished by these writers will be most easily understood, if we examine their procedure by an example, selecting Schumpeter's Theory of Economic Development[1] as a means of demonstration. Schumpeter's basic idea is to complete the usual concept of a static state which describes equilibrium and small marginal variations by a " theory of capitalist change ". He builds up this dynamic system by combining the general data of an exchange order with some particular conditions, such as the existence of different types of economic men, of a specific kind of technique and organization effecting large and discontinuous alterations in the use of the existing productive factors, and finally of a credit system which makes for the financing of technical progress. This order of data once assumed, the market process deduced from them takes on a form which is very different from the classical moving equilibrium. By utilizing the existing technical and financial opportunities, the active group among the entrepreneurs brings about a rise in general business activity which gradually develops into a boom, but ultimately turns into the competitive fight of crisis and depression. This eliminates the marginal producers and effects a redistribution of industrial

[1] Recently published in English by the Harvard University Press. See also his paper on " The Instability of Capitalism " (*Economic Journal*, vol. xxxviii, Nr. 151, pp. 361-86).

fortunes, paving the way for a recapitulation of the same process.

Obviously this analysis of technical progress implies more than the explanation of some special phenomena of the industrial system, and even more than a general theory of the trade cycle. It aims at the interpretation of industrial evolution as a whole and of its dynamic transformation. But at the same time the " intrusion into theory of views savouring of sociology "[1] cannot be doubted. The particular subjective and objective elements on which the deduction of that unstable circular flow is based represent essential features of the social organization of industrial production during a definite historical period. Therefore the methodic procedure is the same as with the classical writers : the introduction of one or more sociological middle principles into the general categories of the exchange economy, and the derivation therefrom of a determinate system of substantial relations and objective processes. The fundamental difference between such an attempt and Marshall's cannot be overlooked. Where he starts within the classical framework, modifying the details according to the circumstances of every individual case, Schumpeter—" before taking account of the full complexity of the ' real ' phenomenon "[2]—starts with the substantial reconstruction of the ground-plan, believing that every historical epoch has a

[1] Schumpeter, " The Instability of Capitalism " (*Economic Journal*, vol. xxxviii, Nr. 151, p. 379n).

[2] Schumpeter, op. cit., p. 383.

general structure which can be described as soon as the adequate middle principles are discovered.

Selecting these middle principles, determining their relative importance and arranging their order, is certainly a task for sociology. All these modern deductions of the total process of the industrial market we glanced at, though mainly presented by economic specialists, imply a sociology of the modern world embodied in reasoning on prices and volumes of services and commodities. Methodological awareness of these connections is required by the mere fact that up to the present the realistic theorists have not agreed on the social key-positions of the industrial system. Beside the rectification of paralogisms, only elucidation of these sociological premises will transfer discussion into those fields where the validity of the differing conceptions can be ultimately tested. Therefore Oppenheimer was thoroughly consistent when he gradually built up a whole system of sociology in order to account for essence, origin and verificability of his middle principles.

In the same way the institutionalists were right in their attempts at revealing the latent preconceptions of some orthodox doctrines. But they cast away the good with the bad when they rejected also the traditional method of reasoning. Discovering the sociological principles of Western industrialism is only the first step for the realistic theorist. As long as these premises persist in the qualitative form in which sociological research brings them to light, he cannot use them any better than the classical writers were able to use the subtle psychological reflections of Hobbes or Montaigne. His analytical work only starts when he does with the complicated material of modern sociological investigation what the classical writers did with their simple preconceptions: transforming them into computable magnitudes and relations. It does not mean very much for the explanation of the market process, if we state that positions of social power influence the functioning of exchange. Only after having transformed that sociological finding into the concept of monopoly, thereby expressing a qualitative structure of social relations by means of a quantitative order of prices and volumes, do we understand the *economic* significance of social power. In his *Purchasing Power of Money* Irving Fisher has based his explanation of the trade cycle partly on a peculiar mental constitution of the bankers. This statement first of all merely relates to social psychology and may there find its causal explanation. It became an economic element only when Fisher expressed it in terms of the supply schedule of money capital, of an increase or decrease of the rate of interest. Similarly political intervention as an economic datum means deflecting particular prices and quantities from the calculable level they are tending to, if we leave them to the free forces of the market. And a change of technique is an economic phenomenon as far as it is concerned e.g. with the substitution of certain productive factors for others, or with a change in the velocity of adjustment.

IV

With that our primary question as to the exactness of the quantitative relations ascribed to the modern market arises again. It is certainly more than a merely subjective equilibrium of individual valuations which is formulated by the realistic theorists in their statements of the modern circular flow. But obviously they are dealing with phenomena which are much more complicated than the simple movements and relations of the classical system. New analytical instruments are required in order to describe and explain the slowness of the individual adjustment, the numerous cross-currents between simultaneous movements, the large and sudden changes in the circular flow as a whole. Acceleration and retardation, lag and dispersion, superposition and generalization express the objective characteristics of a state in which the economic subjects cannot restrict themselves to mere "reacting", but are constantly "anticipating" from "expectations" rather than from knowledge, bearing "risk" and "uncertainty" for the sake of "entrepreneurs' profit" and basing their calculations on the point of "minimum loss" rather than of coincidence between money costs and price.

All these conceptions are very inexact, if we want to calculate the future point of rest in any market movement. But it is not only the possibility of a clash between the actual point of rest and the calculable point of objective equilibrium which makes modern deduction less determinate than the classical laws. Even more important is the fact that the point of rest as such is no longer of primary interest. The essential difference between classical and modern reasoning consists in a shifting of research from state to process, from the lasting constellations of rest to the varying course and shape of the movements.

This alteration of the principal question has been caused by the alteration of the empirical outlook. As we have seen, the whole classical analysis was based on the supposition that all movements in the market are nothing but short run interruptions of a state of objective equilibrium, and therefore negligible if the fundamental order is to be studied. But the actual form and duration of the market movements prevents us from giving them the status of mere frictions. As a rule there are no small and short vibrations compensating each other by a process of equilibration. The growing immobility of the agents of production and the incessant technical reorganization evoke one-sided and long-lasting aberrations from any starting-point which never come back to real rest and sometimes do not even tend to. Certainly the famous " ceteris paribus " method which follows up any individual movement from rise to rest has not lost all importance. But while under the classical assumptions this working rule had a realistic significance—other things in fact remaining equal during the course of a mere short run friction—its present significance is only instrumentalistic. It aims at isolating any long-lasting movement by an imagined elimination of all simultaneous events in other parts of the system which probably might influence and deflect the process under consideration. Examining the hypothetical point of rest of such an isolated movement will help us to estimate vigour and direction of one among the whole nexus of active forces but never to reproduce the real process. It is only by dropping the classical misconception that objective equilibrium and states of rest are the true subjects of research, that some modern theorists have been able to cope with their task at all. It is the various forms of disequilibrium, the entanglement of simultaneous movements and the sequence of varying constellations during the course of moving disequilibrium which now comes to the forefront of realistic theory.

It may be asked, however, whether there is any space for theoretical generalizations and calculable rules if once we leave the solid ground of objective equilibrium. Do we not enter the realm of unlimited possibilities, are we not trying to discover the rules of chaos, if equality between money costs and price has gone? This question cannot be answered *a priori*. We can imagine a state of affairs which is nothing but a general medley of antagonistic forces lacking any structure and therefore inaccessible to analysis. But the very fact that the market system still is functioning in spite of many setbacks tells us that industrialism is to classical utopia not as chaos to equilibrium. Closer examination even reveals a strange regularity of the real disequilibrium.

It is the systematic importance of the theory of industrial fluctuations or trade cycles that it has discovered and tried to explain a well-marked rhythm of the disequilibrating exchange process. It started as a special interpretation of an exceptional case, certainly exceptional within the realm of the classical assumptions. But it is moving more and more into the centre of realistic theory. If the theorist once has grasped that in the industrial world no economic phenomenon, no change in demand or supply of commodities or services, ever materializes outside the rhythm of the trade cycle, he ultimately cannot escape the conclusion that here with the fixed sequence of the cyclical phases experience offers him a basis of calculation capable of taking the place of the inapplicable classical concept of equilibrium.

Certainly the form and the exactness of the reasoning on the dynamics of processes largely differs from the analysis of the statics of rest. The system of equations expressing a simultaneous and stable order of prices and volumes is to be replaced by a fixed sequence of definable inequalities which describe typical and recurrent constellations of prices and volumes, at the same time fixing succession and direction of changes and limiting lags and dispersions. We cannot help admitting that as a rule in the real market prices differ widely from the level of money costs, that over more than a short period large masses of factors of production are idle and output is much below its optimum, that in contradistinction to the classical law of supply and demand, all prices usually rise simultaneously and along with increasing production and vice versa. But all these divergences from the equilibrium line do not occur irregularly. We recognize a strict cycle of depression—revival—prosperity—boom—crisis and again depression, and we find typical dispersions between the various movements and a typical order of the whole system in every phase. This basic sequence of the process and these typical constellations within the various phases have not changed over a period of four or five generations, though certainly every individual cycle has its historical characteristics, and though even the process as a whole has undergone some important transformations.

V

The concentration of modern realistic theory on the economic *process* and even on the particular phenomena of the trade cycle need not in itself harmonize the conflicting views of the individual researchers. I have already pointed out that we can hardly speak of a modern realistic system in the sense of a commonly accepted unity of basic assumptions as we can do with classical theory or with modern pure theory. Up to the present there is no such agreement on the essential causes which make for economic fluctuations, as there formerly was on economic man and perfect competition as the conditions of objective equilibrium.

However, even if the internal controversies of trade cycle analysis were settled, and the fundamental causes were comprehended in an authoritative scheme, an ultimate difficulty would still have to be conquered. The point in question will become quite evident, if we remember the conditions for the materialization of objective equilibrium above referred to. We recognized that economic man and competition do not guarantee the existence and persistence of such an equilibrium as long as their efficacy merely relates to the process of exchange itself. Only if these principles are also valid for the process of social evolution as a whole, that is to say, for the changes in birth-rate, migration, saving incentive, technical order, etc., will the movements within the market be protected against distorting influences arising from the social environment; only then will the equilibrating forces definitely prevail. In order to interpret the abstract possibility of a stable equilibrium as the concrete reality of a social order we had to adopt the classical hypothesis that not only the transactions of exchange, but also the social data of these transactions, the supply of labour and capital and the technique of production, are subject to the law of supply and demand and to nothing else.

It is exactly the same with any economic theory of the trade cycle. It remains a hypothetical construction pointing to an isolated market movement unless it is connected with a definite conception of the social process as a whole. To state it in concrete terms : anyone who wants to deduce the trade cycle as the real form of the economic process during the industrial age has to furnish two proofs. He may start by showing that, certain supply conditions of labour and capital, a certain structure of demand and a certain order of technique *given*, e.g. specific methods of credit policy or natural changes in harvest-yield or some other factors evoke a cyclical movement. But he has moreover to show that possible *changes* in those general supply and demand conditions do not distort or neutralize the particular effect of the economic cause of the cycle, and why. Once again the theory of the internal movements in the industrial market must be completed by a theory of the evolution of its social data.

At first sight the prospects of such a theory of social evolution do not look very favourable. The classical hypotheses—law of population, iron law of wages, etc.—which were ingeniously contrived in order to eliminate any distorting influences from outside the market process, have definitely proved to be misconceptions or at any rate unverifiable. Concerning labour supply, we have dismissed any attempt to connect the growth of population with classical economic motives. As far as economic reflections play any role there, they rather tend in the opposite direction combining a decrease in birth-rate with an increase in wealth. To a greater extent migration may be influenced by money incentives though there too more general social forces, established traditions, moral ideas, etc., co-operate.

But even if the number of workers is known, the volume of work still depends upon the relative valuation of work and leisure which varies from individual to individual and even with every individual through time, and which certainly cannot be reduced to simple money calculations. The classical theory of capital supply is in no better plight. Tradition, moral prejudices, etc., in respect of saving, conjectures about future profits which differ from individual to individual appear as more important than the changes in the rate of interest. The technical notions of the early writers are definitely out of date, and as to demand, the true realm of subjective valuations, not even Ricardo tried to deduce its changes from mere money incentives.

Considerations of this kind have more and more induced modern theorists to abandon any theory of the social data of the market, or what amounts to the same thing, of economic evolution, and to take these data as independent variables of their reasoning. This means, of course, that any deduction relating to the internal process of the market lacks ultimate realistic foundation. Our trade cycle analysis and also the more comprehensive modern schemes of the circular flow above mentioned now retain only instrumentalistic significance, as conclusions drawn from hypothetical sociological constellations whose existence and persistence cannot be determined by deductive reasoning. Since the theorist cannot discover any rules for the changes of his general variables, his only refuge is the empirical researcher, the statistician and the historian. They can perhaps supply him with information about the concrete form, magnitude and tendency of his social data, but of course only for the past. Any reliable conjectures as to the future are impossible in principle, and also the economic past as a process is not fully disclosed, but can only be explained from individual and independent causes, and certainly not with the help of general economic categories.

This rather pessimistic result is the logical conclusion drawn from the methodic axiom of the independence of the general market data. The axiom itself, however, though prevailing in modern methodological discussions, does not stand critical examination. Speaking in plain terms, this idea suggests that in the economic world everything is possible, and that in principle any constellation of the data is as probable as any other. But with regard to the past history of the industrial system such a scepticism is absolutely unfounded. The existence of the trade cycle, whatever its ultimate source may be, has entirely changed the causal relations of the general supply and demand conditions. During the last 150 years the significant fluctuations of the supply of labour and capital, of technique and of the general scope and structure of demand have not been produced by the incalculable natural and social factors which influence birth-rate, migration, voluntary saving and the subjective scales of preference for commodities and work. The essential variations of those data have been effected by the course of the trade cycle itself, or ultimately by that factor or complex of factors which first set the cycle in motion and has kept it going during the industrial age.

Among the immense number of logically possible constellations of the data only a few have been realized, and these recur in a typical causal interdependence. These few real constellations are represented by the phases of the trade cycle, every phase including a part of the economic process which is caused by the constellation of the data in the preceding phase, and at the same time producing the new constellation of the data for the economic process in the following phase. Looking e.g. at the constellation after the outbreak of a crisis, we know that the labour market is glutted because of general dismissals, just as the capital market is also glutted owing to the large liquidation of former investments. Intensity and range of demand are falling, and there is no tendency towards technical extension of supply. But it is more than symptoms of a certain phase of the trade cycle which we thus describe. It is at the same time the general data for the following phase of depression and later on of revival. Thus by its very course the industrial circular flow creates a series of typical supply and demand conditions which determine its process as they are determined by it. Certainly during the industrial age many non-typical and " independent " influences—independent of the causal sequence of the cyclical phases—were constantly operating. But obviously these incalculable factors were not strong enough to deflect the calculable rhythm in which the data vary under the influence of the cyclical force, that is to say, of those impulses which arise within the economic sphere itself, if once the cycle is started.[1] Therefore, comparing the relative vigour of independent and dependent forces we may state without exaggeration that in the industrial system the economic process itself produces and changes its data.

These considerations are of great importance, not only for the past. They allow us to predetermine also the future constellations of the data, if we start from two assumptions : (1) that the recurrence of the trade cycle during the last century is not merely a casual event, but due to a homogeneous complex of causal factors, and (2) that this complex of factors will operate also in the future. It is true, we cannot foresee the birth-rate of 1940 except within certain limits. Therefore we cannot estimate to-day how large the natural influx into the English labour market will be in 1954. We certainly do not know anything about the immigration laws at that time and still less about the subjective scales of preference for work and leisure of the individuals under consideration. Nevertheless we are able even to-day to describe the

[1] Closer examination might show that even some of these independent factors (gold-discoveries, harvest yields, institutional changes of the economic order) became more and more implicated in the cyclical rhythm.

possible constellations of the labour market of 1954 and its relation to the other supply conditions and to the order of demand, if our general assumptions as to the causes and to the persistence of the trade cycle are valid. Though we cannot predict which phase of the cycle will prevail in 1954, we need not refrain from making any statement at all. As long as the cyclical forces are operating with unchanged vigour, the number of generally possible constellations is strictly limited, and the order of all these constellations is calculable.

But our result is of even greater importance for the theoretical construction of a realistic scheme of the industrial circular flow. As long as the primary causes of the trade cycle persist, the economic process will produce its own data irrespective of other independent influences. The trade cycle will not be deflected from its typical course, and the fixed sequence of the cyclical phases represents the basic form of the circular flow and the theoretical system of co-ordinates of any realistic analysis.

VI

Now we are able to ascertain the basic relations between sociology and modern realistic theory. Formally they are very similar to the relation between sociology and classical economics. In both cases determinateness of reasoning is secured by inserting some middle principles into the categories of a pure theory of exchange, and in both cases the purport of these principles is a sociological one, pointing to certain objective institutions and subjective rules of conduct which prevail in the society under consideration. What makes the difference is the substance of the respective middle principles, and with that the resulting form of the circular flow.

In the face of the discussions which still are going on between various schools of realistic theory, we refrained from contrasting one particular set of modern hypotheses with the classical idea of economic man and perfect competition.[1] Nevertheless we could discover some general characteristics common to all modern conceptions and fundamentally opposed to the classical view. Suggested by the real structure of the industrial economy, no states of rest and no equilibria, but processes and definable disequilibria have come to the forefront of modern investigation. Dynamic theory more and more tends to construct a new co-ordinate system of realistic research, substituting the regular sequence of the phases of the trade cycle for the classical permanence of equilibrium between money costs and prices. This new turn is to guard modern theory from two

[1] Some remarks as to the positive content of a realistic system of modern industrialism will be found in the following chapters. See also some of my former papers (" Der gegenwärtige Stand der Konjunkturforschung in Deutschland in Festgabe für Lujo Brentano", 1925, vol. ii, pp. 329-77, and "Wie ist Konjunkturtheorie überhaupt möglich ?" in *Weltwirtschaftliches Archiv.*, vol. xxiv, pp. 165-97), and my contribution in *Schriften des Vereins für Sozialpolitik*, vol. 175, pp. 335-47. I intend to deal more explicitly with this main specialist problem of modern economics in a forthcoming publication.

equally destructive alternatives, from unreality as well as from inexactness. For so far as the middle principles depict true features of modern economic society, the analytical results can be verified ; so far as the movements of prices and volumes fit in with the rhythm of the trade cycle, their tendencies are calculable.

Of course in this system of dynamic processes exactness and calculability have a different meaning from what they had in the classical order of short and equilibrating vibrations. On the one hand " deviations " are no longer negligible, but are our main subject of study. On the other hand the deductive scheme of the cyclical phases supplies only the general type and tendency and the limits of lag and dispersion for the various movements. Within this scheme considerable scope is left for the deflecting influences of the particular space and time. Therefore the deductive range of modern theory is necessarily smaller than that of classical theory. We must complete it step by step by empirical research, if we want to differentiate the approximate results of reasoning according to individual circumstances. For this purpose we have to mobilize the whole arsenal of analytical and statistical tools which the instrumentalistic work of the last decades has produced. In this way our empirical research work will prove to be in full harmony with the deductive procedure of realistic theory. Moreover, only within the new co-ordinate system of cyclical phases and not under the fiction of moving equilibrium can our empirical instruments find any point of support at all.[1]

Among the subsidiary branches which thus render modern theory applicable to individual historical constellations, economic sociology in the sense of a descriptive analysis of social institutions and attitudes plays an important role. Therefore it is certainly true that in applied economics "the chain of purely economic analysis is to be interrupted after every link, and a sociological examination of its results . . . is to be inserted".[2] Nevertheless it is not this auxiliary function of making the necessary corrections for individual variations which gives sociology its predominant position in modern as in any realistic economic theory. The economic and the sociological aspect are already combined in the most general statements, because sociological principles necessarily form a part of the categories of realistic economic reasoning.

[1] With the schemes of realistic theory, economics in fact reaches a methodic stage which can be compared with the position of the natural sciences. The sociological middle principles represent something like "ideal constants" of the economic regularities, though they are discovered in a way which is entirely different from the inquiry into natural constants, and though their validity is necessarily restricted to historical epochs. The concrete value of the economic constants of a certain historical order is always modified by the individual circumstances of space and time and is to be determined by econometric research. Cp. above, p. 79.

[2] Heimann, *Sociological Preconceptions*, op. cit., p. 43.

CHAPTER VI

ECONOMICS AND THE SOCIAL TREND OF CAPITALISM

I

It is rather a bald statement that any realistic economic theory is necessarily based on some sociological preconceptions. It is surely more interesting that in the particular case of classical economics, these preconceptions depict more than some discontinuous and accidental features of the underlying social order, that the very structure of the corresponding society can be read in the simple equations of the market laws. The question arises whether the same is valid for the modern analysis of the circular flow. Do the complicated inequalities of dynamic theory equally reproduce the basic forms of a social system, and of what kind of social system?

In classical economics the systematic importance of the middle principles became manifest when we advanced as far as the inquiry into economic evolution, that is to say, to a theory of the social market data. Here, e.g. with the iron law of wages and the theory of saving, was the point where forces whose main field of operation is the transactions of exchange encroached on the social environment of the market. That for some reason the spirit and order of the law of supply and demand are said to prevail also in breeding of children and in the accumulation of private fortunes connects the world of the market with the realm of social biology, with family life, ethical conventions, etc. Modern realistic theory, as we have seen, points to a similar nexus between exchange process and social data. The connecting link is the course of the trade cycle, which determines supply of labour and capital in one phase by the conditions of absorption or dismissal in the preceding phase. Here the linkage appears even stricter in so far as it is the objective constellations of the internal process of the market which control any relevant variations of the external social order. Through the medium of the exchange process the primary cause or causes of the trade cycle, themselves arising from the social environment of the exchange process, react upon that very environment.

In the face of such reciprocal action between social and economic factors, it is hardly possible to interpret the true relation between economics and sociology as a one-sided dependence of economic reasoning on sociological preconceptions. As soon as sociological research passes beyond its supra-historical generalizations on social interrelations as such, and turns to the analysis of a concrete social " system ", obviously it cannot do without economic middle principles. And as in economic reasoning the contribution of sociology is not merely qualifying but fundamental, the theory of the market data suggests that realistic sociology on its part requires economic categories for the most general statements about an order like industrial society. Thus by pursuing our question of the sociological meaning of dynamic economics we may hope to gain also some insight into what economics means for sociology.

II

Even in its loose classical form the idea of a mutual relationship between the economic and the social process has some savour of a materialistic interpretation of history. The role which the trade cycle plays in forming and varying its own social data suggests an even more intimate connection of modern realistic theory with that idea. In this way the course of a purely rational investigation all at once comes upon a conception which generally is taken for a vague metaphysical speculation. But despite the prejudices prevailing among partisans and opponents we shall find at the bottom of this notorious theorem a precise and verifiable working rule.

There is much dispute about the true meaning and the explanatory range of historical materialism. If all metaphysical arguments and hair-splitting definitions are put on one side, in the end the empirical significance of the idea amounts to the claim that the organization of the economic sphere —the " conditions of production "—determines the structure and evolution of the other social spheres. The economic organization itself is said to be subject to periodic transformations according to changes in the " material powers of production ". Therefore the political, legal, and even the artistic, philosophical and religious realms of human activity are ultimately based on the technical order of production whose dynamics necessitates corresponding changes in the social superstructure.

If these statements prove true, economics does not merely play some role in the work of sociological integration, but becomes the centre and foundation of sociology in the widest sense. Nevertheless the pure economists have never welcomed that privilege, because the whole idea apparently contradicts their most elementary statements. The general definition of pure economics : " disposing of scarce means according to given ends " starts, as we have seen, from the supposition that the ends and means of our economic disposal are not themselves problematic, but sheer data of economic analysis. This methodic position in fact expresses a conception of the relation between the economic and the social world generally which is incompatible with historical materialism. It assumes that the natural, social and technical conditions of production arise exclusively from outside the economic sphere, being the cause but never the effect of the economic occurrences under consideration. From this point of view, to reduce the general social process to the economic process is to commit a vicious circle. But in the face of the dynamic effects of the trade cycle, the whole methodological basis of pure theory, namely the idea of " independence of the data ", has proved to be a dogmatic prejudice, which cannot be reconciled with the experience that the economic circular flow transforms its own social environment. It once more makes manifest the fact that from the very outset, pure theory is connected with discontinuous states rather than with continuous processes.

Conversely, the chain of causation as suggested by the materialist concept fits the nexus between the trade cycle and its social data at least formally. Some doubt however arises with regard to the substantial assertion which makes precisely technique the fundamental factor. If technique of production really is to be the ultimate and only determinant first of the economic process and afterwards of social dynamics as a whole, we have to assume that it is the only genuine causal element in our deduction of the circular flow. In that case all the other basic elements of the market, the supply of labour and capital as well as the subjective valuations, become nothing but dependent variables of that very technique. In other words, while up to now we confined ourselves to connecting generally the relevant variations of the market data with the rhythm of the trade cycle, the materialist concept goes a step further and presents us, at least implicitly, with a definite hypothesis on the ultimate source of the trade cycle itself. If we want to test this hypothesis we cannot refrain any longer from entering discussion of the causal origin of the trade cycle. But we shall restrict our analysis to the particular factor under consideration, that is to say, to meaning and importance of technique of production as primary cause of the cyclical process.

III

Technique of production affects the industrial circular flow in a twofold manner. There is on the one hand a continuous influence, arising from the prevailing method by which the various factors of production are technically and hence economically combined, and on the other hand a discontinuous influence, produced by any noticeable alteration in that method. We do well strictly to distinguish between "technical state" and "technical progress" as conditions of cyclical dynamics, because their importance is very different in reality as well as in their contribution to the various theories of the cycle.

The *technical state* of the industrial system is characterized by the prevalence of capital-requiring labour-saving organization of production. Increasing mechanization as such and a growing tendency to substitute mechanical elements for human labour have some social and economic consequences which, as a matter of fact, form an essential argument in every relevant trade cycle theory. If we comprise the vast collection of rival hypotheses under five principal types of causal factors : nature, psychology, money, distribution and technique, closer examination shows that the technical factor dominates analysis even where it is not explicitly mentioned. A mechanical order of production influences the circular flow first of all by the fact that the real, above all, the fixed capital has to be provided before production can start. Therefore, as compared with a technical state in which labour predominates, a high level of industrial technique strengthens the importance of previous accumulation and therefore of the prevailing system of property. In any form of economic society the distribution of property determines the order of consumption. In a system of free exchange the private appropriation of the productive factors cannot but encroach also on the order of production, because the effectual supply of agents of production depends on the free choice of their holders. The early classical writers expected, it is true, that personal freedom, that is to say, free disposal of his labour on the part of every member of the exchange system, might in the end neutralize the inherited inequality of the property order, and might thus eventually secure social stability and social justice. But we have previously pointed out that this social optimism was based on definite technical ideas, particularly on the supposition that labour is and will more and more become the decisive factor of production. It was the revolutionary effect of industrial technique that instead of materializing those utopian hopes, it has actualized and even aggravated the latent possibilities of the existing inequality of distribution as a determinant of production. On the one hand by reserving the access to enterprise to the owners or at least the holders of wealth, on the other hand by weakening the bargaining position of labour by incessant processes of substitution, industrial technique was the creator of capitalism as a social system, and is the natural basis of all theories which connect the trade cycle with distortions in the sphere of distribution.

The necessity of previous accumulation and hence also the prevailing state of technique is at the bottom equally of the monetary theories of the cycle. It is the providing of fixed capital which creates the true problems of investment and of all the monetary and banking manipulations connected with it. But in the monetary hypothesis as in the explanation of the trade cycle from natural and psychological factors, another consequence of modern technique is fundamental. The point in question can be vaguely indicated by the term " immobilization of the circular flow ", and refers to the fact above-mentioned that the prevalence of fixed capital largely influences the amplitude of the oscillations and the velocity of adjustment of the system to changes in the demand and supply conditions. The existence of big sunk costs retards extension as well as contraction of supply, and is the main reason for the long lasting disequilibria between prices and money costs.[1] By that it opens the way to all imaginable distortions and superpositions of market movements and becomes the true cause of the instability of the circular flow. It is this growing lack of response to changing conditions and its cumulative secondary effects to which, after

[1] Historically these problems connected with sunk costs first arose in agriculture, which natural and technical conditions have been felt as a foreign body in the liberal order of the market since the days of Ricardo.

the most elaborate expositions as to the magnetic fields of the planet Venus, or the mental constitution of bankers, all types of trade cycle analysis ultimately have recourse.[1]

This instability of the market process which is produced by the modern technical state as such is very much intensified by the periodical shocks of *technical progress.* To these dynamic interruptions of the static circular flow the technical theories of the trade cycle of Marx or Schumpeter attribute the recurrence of boom and depression. But the argument rightly plays an important role also in the other conceptions. From the outset of industrialism technological unemployment in connection with immobility of real capital has not only effected large distortions in the sphere of distribution, but has at the same time evoked those protective organizations of the labour market which themselves have become new sources of rigidities and distortions. Moreover the acceleration and extension of technical progress during the nineteenth century has exposed the sunk capital to growing risks, and has gradually transformed even the original economic incentive. On the one hand, the desire of securing previous investment has stimulated monopolization, protectionism and imperialistic expansion, creating new problems of social and national distribution as well as new rigidities and distortions of the circular flow. On the other hand, the critical phases of the trade

[1] Cp. for a minute disclosure of latent implications of that kind F. Burchardt, " Entwicklungsgeschichte der monetären Konjunkturtheorie " (*Weltwirtschaftliches Archiv.*, vol. xxviii, pp. 77-143).

cycle always bring about cut-throat competition and later the paralysing process of hoarding, both of them essential factors in the monetary and the psychological theory of the cycle, but ultimately all of them referring to technical state and technical progress.

IV

Having once realized the decisive influence technique of production exerts on modern economic dynamics, we immediately see historical materialism in a new light. It may be doubted whether it can be used as an open sesame for the whole history of mankind. But applied to the analysis of the industrial system it proves an informative working principle. It points to the strange process of self-generation in modern economic evolution which determines the institutional and psychological data of any social constellation in the market by the economic results of the preceding constellation. Far from contradicting the basic statements of realistic economic theory, it draws the final conclusions of the modern analytical findings.

There are two spuriously contradictory elements combined in any cyclical theory of the circular flow. It describes a process which on the one hand is subject to causal compulsion, and on the other hand produces new constellations which alter its own course. But the "reactive" forces restrict the scope of the "creative" forces to such an extent that the progress of transformation is not only slow, but also follows certain rules which are accessible to rational investigation and which are formulated in any economic theory of cyclical evolution. Historical materialism does nothing but transfer this abstract scheme of reciprocal causality between social data and economic circular flow into the concrete process of history, thus revealing the significance of the dynamic middle principle of technique for the social system as a whole.

It describes how, starting with the industrial revolution,[1] this very large scale technique has evoked a process of expansion within and beyond the national borders, which has gradually transformed the economic order, first of the precapitalist age, then of capitalism itself. Under its pressure economic

[1] The causal connection between the industrial revolution and the dynamic process of the trade cycle has been disputed by referring to the existence of economic fluctuations as far back as in the sixteenth century. This objection misjudges the character of those fluctuations as well as the course of the industrial revolution. "There had been many serious periods of crisis and distress for English trade and industry before 1790. . . . In most cases, these were not general, and were closely connected with important political events" (Thorp-Mitchell, *Business Annals*, New York, 1926, p. 150). But it is even more important that the modern investigations of G. Unwin, G. W. Daniels, T. S. Ashton, A. Redford and others have produced full evidence of the fact that the industrial revolution did not arise as a sudden shock, but that the transformation of technique and business organization can be traced back more than three hundred years. Nevertheless, in this process the second half of the eighteenth century represents an exceptional phase which is characterized by the coincidence of particularly numerous and radical changes in all the main sections of industry. In the same period England experienced the first "general" and undoubtedly "economic" trade cycle, a synchronization which as such cannot prove causal connection, but gives as much support to such an hypothesis as an historical comparison possibly can.

man and competition did not produce classical equilibrium but a cyclical disequilibrium as the effect of concentration and immobilization of the material means of production. By economic selection through boom and depression the same forces have also overthrown the precapitalist order of social classes. Mobilizing the immense stock of pre-capitalist wealth for the purpose of industrial investment, technical progress gave with the economic lead also the social and political lead to the owners and disposers of capital. The periodic liquidations superseded not merely an obsolete method of production but whole social classes : the feudal landlords, the traditional farmers, and the middle class of the craftsmen and small traders. Not only have new contracting parties arisen in the market, the large-scale entrepreneur, the financier and the free worker ; at the same time these groups have formed a new aristocracy and a new lower class, enclosing between them a modern type of middle class based on changed economic functions. Finally the rational organization of industrial production became one of the strongest impulses towards a democratic reorganization of the political order and of the educational system, and thus of the modern national state.[1] But this transformation of the social and political strata has also itself reacted on the economic process. The competitive superiority of industrial

[1] See, above all, Max Weber, *Gesammelte politische Schriften*, 1921, and recently Karl Mannheim, " Rational and Irrational Elements in Contemporary Society " (Hobhouse Memorial Lecture, 1934).

technique has been gradually neutralized by the growing risks of investment. A neo-feudal attitude of protectionism is spreading and is using the organizatory forms of the new social and political order for restricting competition. And again the antagonism between the expansionist tendencies of modern technique and the protectionist tendencies of the capital invested in it encroaches on the social and political sphere, checking and even turning back the process of democratic equalization and international integration. Already the final phase of the self-annihilation of industrial dynamics comes in sight: subjection of economic autonomy and free exchange to political regulation and centralized planning.

These aphoristic remarks are not intended as a contribution to economic or social history. They belong to a stage of analysis which should precede any concrete description of historical events and processes. It is the stage where the middle principles of the various periods of civilization become manifest, where the theoretical skeleton of any empirical research of human affairs is formed. There we recognize technique of production to be one of the basic factors in the order and evolution of an industrial society. But even if we want to analyse no more than the dynamic effects of the technical factor on the *economic* process, we must not restrict our analysis to the economic process. Industrial technique brings about a chain of mutual influences between the economic and the social sphere generally of such a kind that any isolation of the economic or political or cultural aspect falsifies rather than illuminates the true causal relations, even within the limits of one of these sections of human activity.

To have stressed this interrelationship against the narrowness of the specialist point of view, to have pointed to the key position of the technical order within the causal nexus, is the real service of historical materialism, considered in its empirical bearing. It guards us e.g. from overestimating the original role banking organization plays in modern economic dynamics, and from tracing back protectionism to the teachings of Gustav Schmoller, though of course these factors too have a due place in the causal nexus. It cautions us against any light-hearted optimism as to the isolated existence of political democracy and discloses the steely kernel of romantic ideologies. Thus we shall find considerable truth even in the most extreme claim of historical materialism that the spiritual spheres themselves cannot remain aloof of the tendencies of the " sub-structure ". It is only a proof for the integrating power of the middle principles of any historical epoch that the large-scale organization of production became the pattern also for civil and military administration during the nineteenth century, that we meet the particular attitude of economic activity in the style of modern art and thought, and even in our everyday manners and in the forms of private life. Georg Simmel had some reasons after all for describing the general lines of modern civilization under the title of a " Philosophy of Money ".

CHAPTER VII

POWER AND ECONOMIC LAW

I

DYNAMIC economic theory, though its generalizations are less simple and even less exact than the classical laws of the market, nevertheless proves to be a rational system of sociology just as Adam Smith's theory was. Distinguished from the original conception of the market by the middle principle of industrial technique, it subjects the social as well as the economic trend of capitalism to its theorems concerning the cyclical circular flow. But as in classical theory so apparently also in dynamic analysis, strictness of deduction is purchased at the price of eliminating all spontaneous activity of the social members. Economic and social evolution is described as an objective and self-generating process to which the individual has simply to conform in his transactions on pain of social and even physical ruin.

This idea of a superhuman nexus of self-acting objective energies is still emphasized, when by a metaphorical phraseology historical materialism often personifies material factors. It is only natural if in opposition to that the question arises whether it is not human impulses and actions which after all form that spuriously objective system. Though certainly the individual can hardly break the spell, it is nevertheless social consent which sustains the system and directs the process. In other words, the existence and persistence of the objective order depends on what results it achieves as to the satisfaction of wants of the representative groups. Their scales of preference and ideologies are the true links in the chain of reciprocal causation. Even if they are not above causal determination themselves, the human atoms of the social system accumulate, transform, emit and receive those energies which keep the historical process working.

Generally it is the inner understanding of the motives involved in any human activity which on the one hand carries the findings of the social sciences beyond the limits set to the natural sciences, and on the other hand distinguishes empirical social research from social philosophy. Concerning the interpretation of the dynamic market process, the task again devolves on sociology, in particular on social psychology, to pilot economics across the dangerous alternative of a schematism inaccessible to inner understanding, and a metaphysics inaccessible to critical examination. We approached this sphere when we previously discussed the significance of the economic man for the determination of the classical laws. We can now be more precise. We have in mind the human impulses which set industrial evolution originally in motion and keep it going to this day. Or formulated in the lines of historical materialism : if we want to make sure of an unbroken chain of causation from technical order in the economic sphere up to the most refined manifestations of culture, we must first of all know, what human forces have brought about that technical order itself and connect it with the " superstructure ".

The popular conception of historical materialism gives us a simple answer by reducing technique like every economic activity ultimately to the "material", or in Brentano's[1] term, to the " absolute " wants, that is to say, wants such as food, clothing, housing, the satisfaction of which conditions the mere persistence of human life. There can certainly be no dispute about the importance of those absolute wants for social organization throughout history and prehistory. Not only does their satisfaction condition the physical existence and the biological growth of every group, it also limits the scope and the social distribution of leisure time, and therefore the opportunities of cultural development.

It is a symptom of the realistic tradition of Anglo-Saxon sociology that it does not consider these plain facts as indelicate or as detracting from the spiritual dignity of mankind. Nevertheless they hardly suffice to explain the exceptional speed and intensity of technical progress in the West during the last centuries. Just because of its universal validity the connection between absolute wants and order of production is much too vague as to interpret the economic and social structure of a particular period in history, and especially of a period in which

[1] See L. Brentano, Versuch einer Theorie der Bedürfnisse, München, 1908.

technical development has stimulated human want rather than has been stimulated by them. Finally the whole distinction between material and " higher " wants does not stand psychological and sociological examination. On the one hand the most spiritual desires of a refined civilization are often precipitated in the forms in which the daily wants are satisfied. On the other hand the dynamic impulses in the capitalist system can hardly be reduced to eating and drinking.

But though it is not finally tenable, formally the conception of material wants is on the right track. It tries to base the economic incentive on the pre-human biological drives which are, at least in principle, limitable. It we substitute for it, following the modern definition of economics, the whole of human wants, the statements of historical materialism become absolutely meaningless. If the arbitrary schedules of consumers' demand ultimately decide upon the technical order of production, all the diffuse and impalpable impulses of the natural and social world invade once more the economic circular flow, and the chain of causation again becomes indeterminate. The rational scheme of a mutual dependence between technical order and social order can be maintained, only if one paramount impulse exists which eclipses and even comprehends all the other impulses, and thus serves as the psychological mediator between the objective processes.

II

The sociological eye of the classical writers discovered a human motive that in fact dominates economic disposal in the capitalist market, using the diverse valuations of the consumers for a determinate and homogeneous purpose. We are once again meeting the " economic man ". But this time it is not a question of that formal rule of conduct whose validity for all partners in the market conditions the very functioning of any exchange system ; we are thinking of the special incentive of a particular group of partners originating in the particular organization of the industrial market. Under the classical supposition of a perfectly mobile market where a multitude of homogeneous members exchange the product of their labour, the effort for maximum money return operates like a traffic regulation. Whoever keeps to it secures his and the general standard, whoever offends against it endangers his and other people's position. But in any case the market as such is nothing but a passage for existing means, entirely neutral as to their social distribution among the market partners. In direct opposition to that conception, the technical conditions of the industrial market have destroyed the social neutrality of the exchange process. Retardation of adjustment and cyclical disequilibrium render the circular flow a permanent mechanism for the redistribution of wealth. Certain differences in the original bargaining power of the partners once given, the industrial process develops into a source of individual enrichment. Thus the maximum money return sought by those who hold the stronger bargaining positions, the entrepreneurs of any kind, turns from an intermediate into a final end: acquisition.

To connect in this way the technical dynamics of capitalism with the bargaining motive of the entrepreneurs certainly furthers our inner understanding of the objective process. But the true nature of this motive itself is still obscure. The usual definition economics offers: profit incentive or acquisitive drive, does not satisfy the sociologist. It describes very well the entrepreneurs' behaviour in capitalism, but it does not interpret it. Striving after wealth generally is a behaviour familiar to almost every historical epoch. As a means for consumption, wealth was even more aspired to in feudal ages. Certainly also the capitalist entrepreneur has a personal demand schedule for commodities and services. But the contraries of consumption and prodigality, namely saving and accumulation, are the striking features of his attitude to wealth—not consuming the cake, as Mr. Keynes has said, but owning and increasing it.[1]

It is from the social consequences of *possessing* wealth and not from the individual pleasure of *consuming* it that we have to interpret the capitalist psychology of acquisition. Though it acts through

[1] J. M. Keynes, *The Economic Consequences of the Peace*, 1919, pp. 16-18.

economic disposals and though it dominates the order and evolution of the economic sphere under industrial conditions, ultimately this impulse does not relate at all to man's original scarcity of means. That it is most pronounced in those individuals who have themselves been most successful in overcoming the stinginess of nature, renders the profit incentive a veritable paradox.

We can solve the paradox only by contrasting the psychological function of accumulation in the capitalist age with the role played by wealth in other social systems.[1] All precapitalist societies placed various forms of direct executive power at the disposal of the privileged groups, thus legitimizing violence, the use and even the abuse of political competence, of legal status, etc., in ways which commonly yielded also material wealth. Liberal society has in principle mediatized social power. It has withdrawn the direct power of man over man from the social élites, and has transformed it into an abstract power of the state, submitted to strict and calculable legal norms. In such an order of political equality only economic inequality can stabilize permanent positions of social power in the hands of private individuals. Likewise the

[1] Cp. Karl Mannheim, "Über das Wesen und die Bedeutung des wirtschaftlichen Erfolgsstrebens" (*Archiv für Sozialwissenschaft und Sozialpolitik*, vol. 63, Nr. 3, pp. 449-512), and F. H. Knight, "The Ethics of Competition" (*Quarterly Journal of Economics*, vol. 37, pp. 579-624). Th. Veblen's *Theory of the Leisure Class*, New York, 1918, though describing secondary features of modern society well, hardly touches its primary dynamic characteristics.

average individuals, formally equal in rights and duties, deprived by army and police of every chance of directly altering their fate, have hardly any other way of social ascent than the roundabout way of acquisition. We can express this in Sombart's[1] antithesis : in every society before the capitalist age social status procured wealth—in the capitalist age only wealth procures social status.

The economic man of the industrial age, understood as the spiritual prototype of modern enterprise, is neither an ordinary hedonist nor an abnormal niggard. His endless striving after profit and accumulation, falsely credited with no substantial end, in fact uses economic transactions for a very distinct aim which formerly inspired the use of political instruments. Since it is not so much lawful ownership as actual disposal and command which serves this end, the transition in the course of capitalist development from individual to corporate ownership has only stimulated that strange substitution of impulses : the use of man's power over nature to give man power over man.

These considerations reveal the ultimate meaning of historical materialism as an empirical working rule. To regard the technical dynamics of the modern process of production as the essential middle principle for the explanation of industrial society as a whole, does not reduce social facts to natural or technical facts, and does not even state a prevalence of the economic world of means over the social world

[1] W. Sombart, *Der moderne Kapitalismus*, 1928, vol. i, chapter 36.

of ends. It only emphasizes the meta-economic significance of the industrial market as the very accumulator and transformer of primary human impulses.

III

Three principles determine order and evolution of the industrial circular flow : the political principle of free association and unequal distribution of private property, the technical principle of large-scale organization and mechanization, and the psychological principle of profit incentive. Though certainly all of them are related to each other by the mere fact that the homogeneous historical process of Western civilization has produced them, the actual state of historical knowledge hardly allows us to reduce their number or to trace them to a single one. The modern political system is an offspring but at the same time the counterpart of the absolute state ; its particular order of property leads back to feudal times, above all to the original appropriation of land. The mediatization of feudal aristocracy, also a political event, initiated the transformation of the power impulse into the profit incentive. Finally mechanical technique and large-scale organization are based on such disparate facts as modern science and the existence of an unpropertied class.

Nevertheless once set in operation, by a nexus of reciprocal causation these three basic factors interlace into the structural unity of a coherent process. They no longer behave as independent variables, they are merged in a self-acting circular flow which reproduces them as its driving forces. Even technique of production, which obviously holds a key-position in the chain of causation, is not exempt from the influence of the other factors and of the economic process as a whole, because execution of technical innovations also depends on the course of the trade cycle. On the one hand the cost and sale conditions of depression stimulate reorganization and the application of new technological findings ; on the other hand the scope of new investment is limited by the amount of free capital available. And it is equally plain that the underlying psychological impulse, whatever its origin may have been, cannot be detached from the causal nexus generally. The circular flow offers only one way of actualizing profit incentive : supplying marketable commodities and services, that is to say, winning the competitive fight for the satisfaction of consumers' demand. Thus the profit incentive induces the entrepreneur to materialize the objective purport of any economic system, though service to the consumer need not be among his conscious impulses, and even must not be so beyond the limits of profitability. At the same time the dynamic rhythm of the process, which means growing opportunities as well as growing risks, and above all the whip of the technical progress itself intensify competitive activity to a life-and-death struggle, all the more as the trade cycle concentrates effectual competition throughout the system on one and the same critical phase.[1] Thus, what at first appears as the most spontaneous impulse, striving after social power and social prestige, is ultimately revealed as a symptom of strongest compulsion.

It is only because even the psychological motive power is seen to be included in the nexus of mutual dependence, that we can understand how in industrial dynamics human impulses and material forces fit into each other. Human activity, it is true, mediates between the various stages of the objective process. But this activity itself materializes in stereotyped forms. The tendency to depersonalization we recognized as the basic constituent even of the harmonious classical utopia asserts itself even more strongly in the life-and-death struggle of capitalist competition. The uniformity of market conduct has not been invented by the theorist for the sake of simple reasoning. It is the dynamic process of the market itself which enforces homogeneous impulses and modes of behaviour on its members. That does not mean that in realistic theory we are to revive that caricature of the economic man who blindly runs after any change in prices or money returns. The real market conduct has passed through several stages of development, from mere reacting to consumers' stimuli to

[1] It was Oppenheimer who first connected the difference between "harmonious" and "cut-throat" competition with the particular structure of the capitalist order. Cp. *Die Siedlungsgenossenschaft*, 1896, pp. 117-46, and recently *System der Soziologie*, vol. iii, pp. 945-61.

anticipating them, from risking capital to protecting it, from harmonious to cut-throat competition. Not only the various historical periods but also the individual social strata of the market partners differ widely in bargaining behaviour. But the changes and differences themselves are accessible to rational interpretation, because they are connected with the structure and transformation of the social system, thus once more confirming the unity of the dynamic process.

IV

In the foregoing exposition we sometimes applied the term " dynamics " to the specific form, in which the industrial process presents itself. Thereby we pointed to those constituents of the circular flow which bring about its recurrence and its transformation. There is on the one hand the chain of reciprocal causation by which the circular flow constantly reproduces the conditions of its continuance, and there is on the other hand the gradual change which the circular flow has to undergo in order to balance the disequilibria of its course. Both of these phenomena though widely differing in their consequences nevertheless form the structural unity of one and the same process which is kept in motion and directed by the combined agency of the three basic factors.

The constant recurrence which makes the circular flow an economic and social system is no peculiar characteristic of the industrial process. We noticed the same autonomy of self-generating forces also in the liberal prototype of the classical system. Conversely, the transforming tendencies of the circular flow are the peculiar feature of capitalist reality and its decisive mark of distinction from liberal utopia. The exposition of the true significance of these tendencies will definitely bring to light the conformity of the economic and the sociological aspect.

The dynamics of structural transformation is, as we have seen, the field of operation of the technical factor. There was private property and an unequal distribution of that property, an abstract medium of exchange, a power impulse and even a self-moving circular flow, before industrial technique arose. But the arrival of this technique actualized for the first time all virtual potentialities latent in these institutional and psychological elements. It has transformed private property into monopoly, money into capital, money incentive into the acquisitive drive and the utopian possibility of a moving equilibrium into the historical reality of the trade cycle. Moreover, once the new order was created, its structural elements themselves were subject to the agency of the same technical factor. They underwent a further transformation whose ultimate tendency is gradually coming to the surface ; reorganization of the Western social system as a whole.

Thus in the end capitalist evolution most impressively confirms our previous results as to the political, technical and psychological preconditions of any economy and society based on free exchange, conditions which are formalized in the middle principles of classical economics ; economic man and perfect competition. The industrial system has not materialized these principles, certainly not perfect competition. It is true that nevertheless capitalism was and is an economic and social system and not a mere aggregate of incoherent bargaining transactions. But it is also true that from the very outset capitalism has lacked stability, at first with regard to internal order but latterly with regard to its continuance generally. Thus the tendencies to self-paralysation which the reality of the industrial system shows, justify our former conclusions: no stable system of free exchange outside the conditions of the classical laws of the market. The less exact laws of dynamic economics depict more than a durationless constellation but less than the continuity of a stable process, and therefore they come as near to reality as scientific analysis possibly can.

In this way again the key-position of the technical factor in dynamic analysis finds its ultimate explanation. Within the nexus of historical reality the technical component is neither superior to nor independent of the political and the psychological component, not even within the autonomous circular flow of the industrial process, as we have seen. Moreover, contemporary history shows an example, Russia, where large-scale technique is not only combined with very different political and psychological principles, but where social dynamics hardly follows any autonomous tendencies of technique.[1] It is only within the particular combination of free association, unequal distribution of private property and profit incentive that industrial technique could develop into the dynamic factor par excellence. But since its action makes for the recasting and even for the dissolution of the original combination, its autonomous operation seems to be transitory even here.

So exceptional and unstable a constellation, looked at from the point of view of history, has become the main problem of realistic reasoning in economic theory since the days of the classical writers. Reality presented them with the question whether and how a society of exchange can be productive and stable, or in methodological terms, with the problem of objective equilibrium. It only shows the thoroughly sociological stamp of economics that this setting of the problem dominates analysis to this day. Market equilibrium or rather the nature of real disequilibrium is the vital question of Western

[1] Another example may be found in the idea of some neo-liberal circles. Their adherents built their hopes on a turn in capitalist technique which might restore or rather for the first time establish free competition and a stable market by reconciling mobility and efficiency. It cannot be denied that the recent development in technology (electromotor) shows some tendencies which will perhaps give a chance to industrial decentralization. The lasting mass unemployment in the industrial countries may even stimulate these tendencies.

Though it is still rather utopian, this idea is at least a useful speculation in order to demonstrate the lability of any structure in the social world and the danger of hypostatizing historical constellations.

civilization now as then. This brings industrial technique rightly into the centre of argument as the very element that makes for disequilibrium and instability. If it came but gradually into the range of theoretical vision, the chief reason was that large-scale organization arose only after the groundplan of the classical system had been constructed on very different technical assumptions. Its retention of these technical assumptions beyond the classical age tended to estrange economic science from economic reality. It is a symptom of their reconciliation that now technique more and more takes the key-position in realistic theory.

But it means also an important step towards a new unity of social research. Modern dynamic evolution enforces co-operation upon economics and sociology because the real chain of reciprocal causation carries the chain of reasoning across any specialist borders. There is no need for abstract postulates of methodology, the trend of thinking is towards integration.

CHAPTER VIII

SOME EVIDENT CONCLUSIONS

I

When discussing some topical matters of economic and sociological research in the preceding chapters, we were raising questions rather than answering them. Nevertheless we are now to cut short substantial analysis. We did not undertake it for its own sake; it was a means of demonstration for a methodological end, namely to illuminate the actual and the true relationship between two sections of the social sciences. We shall now try to summarize our results.

If the social sciences are to cope with the gigantic task which the complexity of modern society sets every specialist, neither economics nor sociology can evade the necessity of modifying to some extent its methods of investigation as well as of teaching. Still it is not so much a question of external reforms like the formation of organizing bodies, the foundation of institutes and periodicals, etc., as of a change of mind and scientific attitude. The most striking symptom of the actual state of affairs is perhaps the lack of contact between the specialists, with its natural consequence, a surprising unawareness among them of what is really going on in the neighbourhood. But new scientific routes will hardly be taken, and more perfect textbooks will scarcely be written before the existing ones are read, and, what really matters, read outside the circles of their origin. The progress within the various special sciences has been so rapid during the last generation that it is by no means sufficient for the sociologist to rely on what he heard of economic theory a generation ago, or for the economist occasionally to look through one of the sociological periodicals printed in his mother-tongue. The particularly national stamp which for obvious reasons marks the social sciences, compels the researcher to look beyond the national borders, the more so because pioneer work is reported in the textbooks only after years and decades. Thus the primary condition of any reform, the spread of knowledge, cannot dispense with constant and personal contact between the specialists themselves.

It is the same with academic education, with the usual curricula, lectures, theses and examination papers. Here, too, the trend towards specialization, inevitable from the professional point of view and in itself perhaps a stimulus to training in method, lacks integration, especially, as we previously observed, in the classical country of synthetic education: England. If there the "literae humaniores" are ever to find their counterpart in an equally organic development of the "Modern Greats", the reconstructed unity of the social sciences must form the basis.

But all these advances cannot be achieved by means of complaint and exhortation. The desire for information beyond the specialist borders must spring out of the daily experience of scholars, teachers and students. As soon as they realize that for the solution of their specialist problems they depend on the kindred sciences, co-operation will start. Therefore the centre of any reform is within the various sections themselves, and the primary means is the individual researcher's awareness as to the sources of his premises and the range of his conclusions. By once more setting up some notice-boards as well as some sign-posts which point to these preconditions of any reform, we shall bring our considerations to an end.

II

How can economics best make use of sociological research ?

(1) Co-operation can take place at two different stages of economic analysis, and at both stages it is an indispensable precondition for any substantial statement.

(*a*) One form of co-operation is concerned with applied economics. Here sociology offers the specific data which adapt the generalizations of economic theory to the particular conditions of space and time. Though, as we shall shortly explain once more, the system of co-ordinates for the descriptive and causal analysis of any economic order is supplied by the realistic theory of the epoch in question—theory of the manorial system, of the liberal market economy, of capitalism, of centralized planning, etc.

—economic theory as such cannot give more than the framework for interpreting institutions and processes, the measures of economic policy and the connection of the economic sphere with the other sections of society. To fill the frame, to render concrete the abstract schemes and working hypotheses is the task of "economic sociology" as described in Chapter II.

This form of collaboration is generally welcomed by the economists and is practised to a growing extent. For some time the danger was imminent that structural and causal analysis might even be overgrown by the sociological material. Now that deductive reasoning has been revived also in the applied spheres of economics, this kind of integrating work is thoroughly satisfactory and constantly improving.

(*b*) The other form of co-operation concerns economic theory. Here the traditional attitude of the economists towards sociology is very different, because the defects of classical economics have prejudiced the whole scientific evolution during the last two generations. The growing lack of realism in classical theory has been imputed not so much to its particular sociological content and method as to its dealing with a sociological, that is, a temporal constellation at all. Not only has pure theory as such arisen as a reaction against the sociological, political and philosophical implications of the classical writers, but this pure theory and the methods derived from it have more and more been identified with theoretical analysis generally.

(2) If this methodic development, which was once started to combat the lack of realism in classical and post-classical economics, is to be preserved from itself endangering the character of economics as an empirical and applicable science, methodological vigilance will be required. The task is twofold, critical as well as positive. On the critical side it consists in demonstrating how narrow the limits and how bald and devoid of substantial meaning are the results of pure reasoning, if we in fact restrict it to supra-sociological generalizations. On the positive side the task is to show that a body of realistic generalizations is possible and already in course of formation which reproduces the general structure and the regularities of motion of particular "economic systems", that is to say, of the historical materializations of a social and economic unity. Though in principle realistic theory is a methodic means of analysing any real or imaginable economic system, for obvious practical reasons the existing models deal as a rule with modern capitalism.

Realistic theory does not rival but completes pure theory. Like classical economics it moves at a lower level of abstraction, intentionally taking into consideration those middle principles which connect the economic with the social process. Nevertheless realistic theory differs widely from applied economics as previously described. It only refers to the integral constituents of the social system in question, not to all the disparate and transitory features of the social environment which make concrete events and individual constellations specific. That is the reason why realistic theory in its various manifestations can succeed in stating causal rules, like the law of supply and demand or the sequence of the trade cycle, generalizations which are certainly not so wide as the supra-sociological statements of pure theory but wider than the findings of applied economics. They are concerned with historical structure and historical laws which represent on the one hand the only objective and determinable form in which the categories of pure theory materialize at all, and on the other hand the framework within which concrete economic actions and institutions individualize and influence each other.

(3) Realistic theory in this sense is no invention of modern times. As we have pointed out again and again, classical theory represents a perfect pattern of this type of analysis, if we judge it by its systematic attempts rather than by its contribution to special problems. But modern realistic theory should differ from the classical pattern above all by its attitude towards the non-economic preconditions of its reasoning, that is, the sociological middle principles. We tried to explain why the classical writers were generally lacking in awareness and critical grasp of their sociological premises, and what is even more important, that the particular constellation they analysed in fact exempted them from accurate distinction between economic and social elements. The society of exchange which they had in mind shows a complete uniformity of impulses and institutions

in all social spheres, so that anyone section like the economic sphere displays the structure and evolution of the whole. It was this representative character of economics under liberal conditions which made possible its scientific autonomy and preponderance during the nineteenth century.

However the conditions for such a simple and lasting congruence between the economic process and the general social process have not come true, whatever the reasons. Thus the picture of the circular flow outlined in classical theory, became incompatible with the facts. This lack of realism of the general conception has damaged the reputation of classical economics much more than analytical defects in the solution of special problems like the theory of value or of interest. But it has moreover damaged the reputation of realistic theory as such. This theory must now be rebuilt on the methodological ground of classical economics rather than on what remains of its substance.

Any realistic theory of the modern economic system must start from the general premise that it can no longer deal with a constant structure and with homogeneous processes, but that the economic order under consideration is subject to an evolutionary transformation. Therefore any deductive operation with invariable data is defective from the very outset. Long period analysis cannot dispense with a previous examination of the tendencies of the data themselves, that is to say, the corresponding sociological constellation and its regular changes, and moreover with the examination of the mutual relations of the variations on both sides. Above all this dynamic chain of reciprocal causation between the economic process and its social environment calls for a theoretical system of co-ordinates which is on the one hand determinate enough to define the course of individual movements, and on the other hand elastic enough to reproduce the regular transformation of the system as a whole. We need not expressly decide henceforth to insert sociological elements into our economic deductions—there was never any substantial statement which was not based on such premises. But we are to render manifest and open to continuous examination and revision those implications which formerly remained latent, and whose modifications were usually neglected.

(4) The practical bearing of such a postulate will be best illuminated, if we once more resume the discussion about what we previously called the "instrumentalistic" method in modern analysis.[1] After the breakdown of the classical system, economic theory for a long time refrained from presenting any more general schemes of the economic process as a whole. Apart from the few generalizations of pure theory which are necessarily too wide a mesh to catch any concrete structure, modern theory up to our own day is mainly preoccupied with casuistic investigations. It picks out imaginable constellations of data and deduces therefrom movements and states of rest under varying hypotheses. Any such

[1] Cp. above, pp. 78-80, 88-89, 94-95.

constellation implies a set of sociological premises. But the conditions of the origin and persistence of these constellations are intentionally disregarded, and equally their connection with the system as a whole and any influences which might arise from outside the particular set of data under consideration. For the sake of argument the isolation and continuance of the initial constellation simply are assumed.

The great value of this procedure for the illumination of special movements within the system cannot be doubted, and there has not yet been discovered any other method of partial analysis which could be substituted for it. We call it instrumentalistic, because it does not directly depict real structure, but tries to build up possible types of market orders by pursuing individual movements under the assumption of a typical constellation of the whole. But here arises the main objection. We must know beforehand what constellation of the real market process as a whole is typical, if our instrumentalistic deductions are to have any chance of being applicable. Two practical examples will demonstrate the difficulty in question better than methodological discussion.

(*a*) The prevailing opinion among theorists as to the long run effects of labour-saving technical innovations on employment is still generally optimistic. Provided that the labour market is flexible, any initial displacement is said to be compensated in the short run either by the secondary effects on the wage-level or by new investments introducing further technical innovations. The argument is typically instrumentalistic in so far as on the one hand it isolates innovations within a small section of the market or even within a single business unit, and on the other hand it assumes the persistence of the initial constellation, that is to say, assumes " normal " conditions in the other sections of the system. It is usually stated that just this isolating procedure secures the general validity of the conclusion which now can be inserted into any imaginable constellation of the general circular flow and modified according to its changes. But closer examination reveals a strong prejudice in this argument. It is by no means true that the deduction referred to is " neutral " as to the order of the circular flow as a whole. It presupposes a moving equilibrium in which now and then technical innovations arise, effecting only small deviations from the normal level of employment which can be adjusted in the short period. The assumed conditions exclude precisely the real constellation which is characterized by the recurrent concentration of all essential innovations on the period of recovery, and by a general dismissal of labour throughout the system in the moment of crisis. Thus the real constellation lacks just those elements which make for short run compensation in the instrumentalistic deduction : equal distribution of innovations through time and small deviations from the normal level of employment.

(*b*) Discussing investment, the traditional concept of marginal productivity starts from the assumption that real saving occurs and is transferred to investment continuously and under the conditions of an equilibrating system. For the sake of isolating one single movement, labour is supposed to be fully employed, the order of demand to be stable, and technical innovations are excluded. This constellation is logically possible, but has hardly ever occurred during the industrial age. The voluntary restriction of private consumption, called saving, may happen under any constellation and at any time. But it is practically utilized for investment only under two well defined constellations which differ fundamentally from the data of the instrumentalistic analysis. On the one hand durable consumption goods are formed and previous industrial credits are consolidated under the conditions of depression. On the other hand industrial real capital is newly constructed during the upswing. But it is precisely the typical feature of these constellations that several movements take place at the same time, influencing, stimulating and deflecting each other. Not only are the conditions on the labour market necessarily unstable; the investments of the upswing are essentially connected with a shifting and a distortion of the productivity curve and likewise of the demand curves. Again the basic assumption of the instrumentalistic analysis, namely the existence of an equilibrating and passive system which adjusts itself to the variations of one single factor, misses the very essence of the real dynamic motion.

It cannot be denied that the sets of data which instrumentalistic analysis has picked out in the cases referred to are logically possible, and that a conclusive deduction drawn from these data produces logically correct results. But since this casuistic method confines itself to taking the data as given and to disregarding their position in the circular flow as a whole, it is debarred from establishing anything about the practical importance of its results, and even from guaranteeing that it will find out the real constellation at all among the infinity of possible ones.

Besides these practical doubts, it would be entirely wrong to attribute the failures of instrumentalistic analysis to accidental mistakes in selecting the data. The bad choice in the cases referred to displays a marked consistency which can be illustrated from almost every problem of general interest, and which became manifest only recently in the discussions about the actual world depression and the means of overcoming it. It lasted several years until orthodox economics acknowledged the simple fact that the conclusions drawn from the analysis of credit expansion in an equilibrating system need not be valid *a priori* for the entirely different constellation of a depression. It was not the final conclusions but only the analytical legitimacy of a certain set of data contrary to the "normal" assumptions, which had to fight for recognition.

Here it becomes obvious that instrumentalistic analysis, as it must necessarily be treated in the face of the immense number of logically possible constellations, cannot be "neutral", that is to say, independent of a general concept of the circular flow.

Isolating a special set of data and assuming that it will persist without interference from the other sections of the system implies a very definite idea of the structure of the economic process generally. It is based on the concept we previously called "objective equilibrium", that is, on the assumption of a political, technical and psychological order which reduces all deviations to small, short, sectional frictions without any superimposed influence from simultaneous processes in other parts of the system and above all from the evolution of the system as a whole. Far from producing pure theory by its methodic procedure, instrumentalistic analysis is always steeped in a definite set of general sociological middle principles. In the practical cases under examination these are the familiar principles of the classical system, and we understand at once that the most penetrating conclusions from these data are no more realistic than these data themselves are.

These arguments are not directed against instrumentalistic research as such. They are directed only against applying it without explicitly referring to the system of co-ordinates to which it is related, that is to say, to the structure and evolution of the circular flow within which the special process under consideration occurs. After all it is not possible to deal with every imaginable economic constellation under all imaginable general social conditions. And even if it were practically possible, we should still require a criterion by which to separate the real and relevant cases from the fictitious and negligible ones. If economic theory is to be preserved as an empirical science and not to degenerate into an idle play of formal logic, we have to abandon in instrumentalistic analysis the traditional and certainly comfortable working rule of "other things taken as equal", and to supplant it by a more realistic hypothesis which describes "how things in general change" and interfere with the things under consideration.

(5) To elaborate the system of co-ordinates applied by instrumentalistic analysis and by any other kind of concrete analysis is the task of realistic theory. It will thus give its answer to three main problems of procedure which preoccupy all methodological discussions in economics, the solution of which is a precondition of any satisfactory substantial work :

(*a*) The relationship between the various levels of theoretical abstraction. Between the level of highest abstraction contriving generalizations valid for any economic phenomenon under any natural and social conditions, and the level of highest concreteness dealing with individual constellations, an intermediate level exists at which the general scheme of any imaginable economic system can be reproduced. Here the economic generalizations of the level of highest abstraction are combined with those sociological principles which depict the essential constituents of the social economy under consideration and follow up their variation and transformation. The construction of such schemes is not one theoretical task among others but the indispensable precondition of all causal or descriptive analysis of individual constellations.

(*b*) The position of the data. Specialization in science makes it unavoidable that each branch shall deal only with a limited aspect of the totality of experience, and that it shall take the other aspects as data in its research. Therefore facts which are problems for some other sciences, are in economics to be taken as granted in respect of their existence and structure. Nevertheless it is a dangerous prejudice to handle these data as given once for all, as independent variables, about whose immanent tendencies the economist need no more trouble himself than a worker at the moving band need look to the movements of his neighbour, before he does his part. This procedure is appropriate only to short period analysis. If long period movements and final constellations are to be examined, the autonomous tendencies of the several data and their contact with the process under consideration are to be investigated in coincidence and in constant confrontation with the special deduction.

The basic scheme of realistic theory supplies the special analysis with the typical order of the general data, the types and the sequence of their changes and the various forms of concatenation between social data and economic process. These forms and tendencies differ widely in the various economic systems of history, even in the various kinds of exchange systems. It is a fundamental theorem of realistic theory that under the particular social conditions of the industrial system, data and process are involved in a regular and continuous interaction which makes any concrete constellation, and therefore the system as a whole, essentially unstable and liable to transformation. For this reason in any long period analysis concerning the industrial system, on principle the data are to be handled as " dependent variables ".

(*c*) The meaning of exactness. We have realized that from the very outset economic theory has a quantitative side and a certain affinity to mathematical forms of thought. From the point of view of reproducing the structure of reality, this formal exactness is in itself no superiority and certainly no postulate, but is appropriate because and as long as it corresponds with the real substance of analysis. What is more important, this quantitative exactness is not hostile to the suggested synthesis of economic and sociological elements but, as we have seen, is positively based on it. Exact calculation of economic movements and reproduction of the exchange process by a system of functional equations is possible only within one definite and very exceptional social order, and here it is just the sociological middle principles which transform tautologies into substantial statements.

Because of their sociological origin these transparent equations cannot express the structure of any economic system whatsoever. It is explicable in view of past and present experience that in spite of this many economists are opposed to entering into sociological considerations at all, and passionately desire to retain the formal exactness of the equilibrium system. But they are wrong in attributing the vague and obscure results of some "sociological" economists to the substance rather than to the method of their reasoning. We previously emphasized the fact that the sociological raw material must be transformed into quantitative units and relations, before it can serve the task of determining and specifying economic analysis. It is the omission of this intermediate stage of research and the combination of qualitative description with quantitative deduction, not their attention to sociological facts as such, that has spoiled much of the work of the historical and institutionalist schools. But once the sociological elements are adapted to the economic order, it only depends on the structure of the reality under consideration, how simple or how complicated the resulting quantitative relations are. As long as economics claims to be an empirical science, the exactness of its theoretical generalizations will be judged only by their congruence with the facts. Whatever it may lose in mathematical elegance, its capacity to depict modern reality and to explain its causal concatenation will increase to the extent to which it uses the results of sociology for the constructions of its foundations.[1]

[1] That the methodological position as expounded above and even the solutions proposed are not restricted to economics, but are valid for all the social sciences has been demonstrated by K. Mannheim, *Mensch. u. Gesellschaft im Zeitalter des Umbaus*, Part III.

III

What has sociology on its part to do in order to promote co-operation with economics?

(1) Its function is first of all that of a mediator. In order to provide the economist with the data of his work—with the basic middle principles of realistic theory as well as with the specifying facts of applied economics—the sociologist has to collect all the informations concerning economic matters which the specialist sections of social research produce. By combining the relevant results of social psychology, anthropology, law, political science, etc., economic sociology should be established on a much broader basis and in permanent contact with the progress of economics itself and with its varying questions.

Though sociology's aid as mediator is absolutely indispensable and the very starting-point of fruitful co-operation, this is not sufficient. Concentration of the economist's interest merely on the individual points of linkage with sociological investigations may even be dangerous. The various sections of economic research differ widely in their dependence on sociological elements, and in every analysis we find some parts in which the flow of deduction need not be interrupted by continuous reference to the premises or by verification of the results. Thus the economist might be tempted to focus his attention only on such sociological facts and relations as impinge directly on a particular economic problem, and that only on occasions in which he cannot continue the investigation in hand without overstepping his specialist boundaries.

If we look back, however, upon our previous substantial expositions, we at once realize that such a casuistic method must fail. Fundamental topics like the significance of the producers' incentive for capitalist dynamics, or the influence of technique on the mobility of market elements will hardly gain their full importance for the economist, if he traces their effect only from case to case within some specialist deduction. The range of action, the historical variability and the reciprocal interdependence of economic and other social phenomena which we have had to emphasize again and again, only come fully into view from a more comprehensive standpoint at some distance from the economic sphere as a whole. If he wants to recognize the true points and specific forms of interlacement, the place taken by economic research within the whole of the social sciences and its varying importance in different historical epochs, the economist cannot dispense with a conception of the social process in general. His very utilization of the concrete material which the kindred specialisms offer, implies a hypothesis of how social order and social evolution as a whole are being formed and transformed.

(2) Thus quite spontaneously the work of "synthetic sociology"[1] becomes of primary importance for co-operation. Here, however, another difficulty arises. For good reasons, the comprehensive

[1] Cp. above, pp. 29-30.

pictures, which synthetic sociology has outlined in the past are not very popular with the economists. In most cases they oscillated between two extremes, a mere compilation of facts and a mere speculation on ideals. But neither a sociological encyclopaedia like many recent American publications, nor philosophical constructions on the lines of Hegel or Spencer will give the economist what he urgently wants : insight into the structure of real society—into the structure, not merely the disconnected atoms, into the real order, not mere figments and postulates.

The practical difficulties in achieving a scheme which depicts structure as well as reality have induced many specialist researchers, both within and without the borders of economics, to reject outright any such attempt at synthetic sociology, and to rely on their own critical judgment. But the fallacies of this procedure are obvious. It is sheer self-deception to think that one can advance one single assertion about any part of society without implying a statement on the order of the whole. We need not recapitulate the many illustrations of this plain fact given in the foregoing exposition, from the law of supply and demand to the theory of the trade cycle. Unfortunately there is, it seems, no invisible hand which brings the specialist conceptions of the whole or even of the borderlands into harmony with each other. The economist simply laughs at the notion commonly held by the average lawyer of the operation of the price system. But the anthropologist regards the economist's traditional ideas of working incentives as not less crude. We have to realize that there is only the choice between an unconscious conception of the whole on the basis of common sense with all its obscure fallacies and prejudices, and a scientific working hypothesis with its obvious insufficiencies which are at least accessible to correction in the face of new and inconsistent facts.

Here the synthetic work of sociology has its place. In this task which is not merely scientific but positively ethical, no substitute for it is possible. Among other things it brings into the light of rational criticism the infinity of traditional preconceptions which ebb and flow about the nature of man, the destiny of mankind, the eternal qualities of women, the psychological conditions of an economic system, the necessity of social inequality, and so on. Contrasting those prejudices with each other and with the scientific results of the competent specialism, sociology could achieve a work of enlightenment comparable only to the great victory over superstition with regard to nature.[1]

But at this point it has already become clear that it is the large stores collected by the specialized sciences, not fantastic ideas or arbitrary constructions of its own which are the legitimate sources of the synthetic schemes of sociology. This work requires a critical faculty applied to the selection and

[1] Here is the main field and the true justification of the work, sociology of knowledge has started in recent years. Cp. above all the writings of K. Mannheim, in particular his article " Wissenssoziologie ", in *Handwörterbuch der Soziologie,* Stuttgart, 1931.

combination of specialist results, and an elasticity of mind which never misuses any formula by elevating it into a metaphysical dogma, but keeps strictly to the idea of a working hypothesis, holding the door always open to alternative suggestions and refraining always from being cleverer than the facts.

(3) Among the various sources upon which synthetic sociology draws is of course economics. Economics thus gives back in some measure what it receives from sociology for its own completion. In every epoch of human civilization, economic forces and institutions have deeply influenced the structure and evolution of society as a whole. But in modern history the economic process is, as we have seen, the dominant factor. The laws of exchange form the warp of the social texture; the expansion and transformation of the market reflects the growth and reorganization of the Western communities. At the same time this preponderance of the economic factor has extended the range of social organization as such. The technique of the industrial age has broken through the traditional borders between the social and the natural world and has subjected more and more sections of organic and inorganic nature to human influence. This expansion, however, has reacted on the psychological and institutional constituents of modern society in a strange way. The more nature has become socialized, the more society has become naturalized. In saying this we refer once more to the quasi-natural laws which express by rational formula the stereotyped forms of

conduct and the calculable concatenation of human actions and reactions in modern civilization.

The key-position which the economic factor thus holds as connecting nature and society in the modern world, is reflected by the predominant role which the methods and results of economic research play in synthetic sociology. The main *subject* of any constructive synthesis of modern social history consists on the one hand in disclosing the economic background of attitudes and organizations even where " disposal of scarce means " is not directly involved, and on the other hand in pointing out the constant interactions of all the social factors in the transformation of the structure as a whole. The *methodic* significance of modern economics for sociology is no less important. In the first instance the exceptionally rational method of economic theory only depicts the structure of its particular object. But its tendency to strict causal investigation and the stress it lays on the interdependence of partial processes and individual phenomena makes it ultimately a pattern even for those specialisms of social research whose objects resist quantification and exclude mathematical forms of presentation. Thus economic theory can help the social sciences to overcome finally a foible inherited from their speculative origin, namely its reliance upon analogies and morphological parallelisms, where concrete causal analysis is needed.

(4) However, though the methodic significance of economics for sociology may well be permanent, the

primary importance of its substance, that is to say the preponderance of the economic factor in society as a whole, will probably be transitory. Given the particular political, technical and psychological constellation of industrial society, its order and evolution may follow a " natural law ". But this constellation itself has not been produced by a natural law. Very exceptional conditions which happened but once in human history, have brought it about, and are also tending to transform it in the very process of its historical unfolding.[1] Even during the capitalist age, uniformity of order and rules of motion have largely varied according to the resistance which the previous structure of national unities and social strata have offered to industrial dynamics. Therefore any attempt on the part of economics to usurp the position of sociology in presenting the synthetic scheme of social analysis would misrepresent the facts even of capitalism. But such a pseudo-synthesis would be a positive obstacle to scientific insight, the further the actual trend of Western society progresses. The economic structure will certainly never lose importance for the general social order. But unless all symptoms prove fallacious, the key-positions and the centres of power

[1] To disentangle the complexity of the original conditions of Western civilization and to follow up their development was the main object of the pioneers of modern synthetic sociology : Max Weber, Werner Sombart, Franz Oppenheimer. See the latest and most comprehensive scheme of constructive synthesis in Oppenheimer's " Abriss einer Sozial- und Wirtschaftsgeschichte von der Völkerwanderung bis zur Gegenwart ", *System der Soziologie*, vol. iv.

in the approaching epoch of social history will be based on administration rather than on acquisition.

Thus the time may come when economics will be relieved from its advanced post, perhaps by political science whose substance and methods, somewhat indefinite up to the present, will certainly develop with the development of its task. But even a shifting of the centre of gravity within the social sciences cannot reduce the primary significance of their co-operation, so long as each of them in its own special work continues to pursue the only legitimate aim of any empirical science : that of reproducing the structure of reality.

For Product Safety Concerns and Information please contact our EU representative GPSR@taylorandfrancis.com
Taylor & Francis Verlag GmbH, Kaufingerstraße 24, 80331 München, Germany

www.ingramcontent.com/pod-product-compliance
Lightning Source LLC
LaVergne TN
LVHW021037011026
849160LV00009BA/681

* 9 7 8 0 4 1 5 6 0 7 9 8 8 *